LEGENDS OF WARFARE
AVIATION

Avro Lancaster

RAF Bomber Command's Heavy Bomber in World War II

RON MACKAY

SCHIFFER MILITARY

4880 Lower Valley Road   Atglen, PA 19310

Designed by Justin Watkinson
Type set in Impact/Minion Pro/Univers LT Std

ISBN: 978-0-7643-5845-6
Printed in China

Published by Schiffer Publishing, Ltd.
4880 Lower Valley Road
Atglen, PA 19310
Phone: (610) 593-1777; Fax: (610) 593-2002
E-mail: Info@schifferbooks.com
www.schifferbooks.com

For our complete selection of fine books on this and related subjects, please visit our website at www.schifferbooks.com. You may also write for a free catalog.

Schiffer Publishing's titles are available at special discounts for bulk purchases for sales promotions or premiums. Special editions, including personalized covers, corporate imprints, and excerpts, can be created in large quantities for special needs. For more information, contact the publisher.

We are always looking for people to write books on new and related subjects. If you have an idea for a book, please contact us at proposals@schifferbooks.com.

Photo Credits

Chris Liddle
Mark Postelthwaite
Simon Parry
Jerry Scutts
John Mackintosh

Contents

Introduction

The creation of a comprehensive and strategically effective Royal Air Force (RAF) Bomber Command was beginning to take form during the mid-1930s. The Air Ministry was cognizant of the salient fact that the switch from fabric-covered biplanes with fixed undercarriages to metal-clad monoplane structures incorporating enclosed bomb bays and rotating mountings for defensive weaponry was vitally necessary for any real prospect of striking an adversary's industrial heartland in sufficient manner to disable its capacity to sustain its military forces in the field.

Specification P13/36, issued in September 1936, requested an all-metal twin-engine monoplane of a high-performance nature; this contrasted with its July-issued predecessor, B12/36, whose terms anticipated a design capable of bombloads up to 12,000 pounds. The Avro Company's tender (type 679), submitted in January 1937 for the latter, ironically anticipated an aircraft whose bomb-carrying capacity, for one thing, would place it into the future heavy category, as would its ultimate armament tally of eight machine guns. Against these positive aspects was the unconscious counterthreat to overall performance posed by the power source, the Rolls-Royce Vulture—a sadly prescient name, as operational events would confirm.

What would be Rolls-Royce's rare production failure comprised two Peregrine engines' cylinder blocks mounted on a common crankcase; a 90-degree angle between the blocks gave an "X" cross section appearance. The then-current parallel development of what was an untried power plant with its intended airframe meant that the catalog of technical problems that was being cast up boded ill for its successful assignment to what was named as the Avro Manchester.

In retrospect, it seems illogical that the Avro hierarchy, having become aware of the potentially perilous situation facing their two prototypes awarded under the Air Ministry Contract as well as the production run, still persisted with the Vulture, especially as they were already seeking alternative engines involving the Bristol Company's Hercules and Centaurus radial engines. Be that as it may, the marriage of the Manchester and Vulture went ahead. (The beneficiary both from Rolls-Royce and Bristol sources would be the Manchester's successor, the Lancaster, which itself would be a development emanating directly from its handicapped predecessor!)

The Manchester's airframe more than fully matched up to Spec. P13/36's requirements. The core substructure involving the center fuselage and inner wing sections was cruciform in layout and accordingly solid in basic strength. Further strength was added in the form of twin-wing main spars that were extended into the outer wing sections right up to the wingtips. The nose and rear fuselage were separate subframes.

The 8,000-pound-maximum bombload was confidently increased by Avro to 12,000 pounds; the single-cell bomb bay, extending along marginally less than half the 69-foot, 6-inch fuselage length, was deemed necessary to accommodate two 21-inch torpedoes as demanded within the specification's terms. As a consequence, not only could the largest bomb then in the RAF's arsenal at 2,000 pounds be comfortably stowed, but the introduction during 1941 of the 4,000-pound "Cookie," followed by 8,000- and 12,000-pound successors, would be equally accommodated.

The previous decades of the RAF's existence and its dependence on single flexible gun mountings were steadily albeit not comprehensively becoming a thing of the past by now. In their place had arrived the power-operated gun turret with Plexiglas covers. In the Manchester's case, defensive firepower initially involved Nash and Thompson power turrets that then gave way to similar units from Fraser-Nash (FN). Nose and tail turrets were a mandatory feature from the beginning and were destined to be

The Lancaster's predecessor was the twin-engine Manchester. The basic airframe was similar in layout but with a shorter 90-foot wingspan, smaller-diameter main wheels, and an initially different fin and rudder structure. This is the prototype, L7246.

supplemented by the mounting of a dorsal turret; a ventral gun mounting was also available directly behind the bomb bay, but this was not proceeded with.

The original layout of the tail control surfaces on L7476 involved stabilizers spanning 28 feet, to which were attached twin fins and rudders of relatively small dimensions. In addition, the wingspan measured 80 feet, 2 inches. The second prototype, L7477, featured the addition of a fixed fin on the fuselage and a 9-foot, 11-inch extension to the wings, both measures intended to counter incipient instability experienced during its predecessor's flight test sequence. A further refinement was the inclusion of the gun turrets compared to L7476; to the Nash and Thompson twin-gun nose and tail-mounted units was added a ventral turret, which was never to be utilized on production airframes.

The flight testing of the two prototypes spanned the period from July 1939 to mid-1940. Surprisingly, considering neither airframe nor engines had been fully tested, production of the first 200 out of 300 airframes, ordered in two batches between late 1937 and 1939, had commenced within months of L7246's initial flight on July 27, 1939. However, the former stated production figure would never be exceeded (198 airframes in total) due to the Vulture's inherent problems. However, Sir Roy Chadwick (chief designer) was, by April 1940, actively providing the grounds for a four-engine version, the Manchester Mk. III. As it was, his submission to the Air Ministry that the Merlin be the intended power source was not immediately granted priority, on the basis of the fact that the Rolls-Royce engine was urgently required for Fighter Command's duo of fighters, the Hurricane and Spitfire.

A worse potential blow occurred in July 1940, when Avro was told to drop the proposed four-engine Manchester III variant and turn to producing the Handley-Page Halifax, one of two four-engine bombers now in planned production. Fortunately, Chadwick was able to dissuade the authorities of the switch. An even more vital turnaround by the Air Ministry hierarchy was the agreement to gain resume planning for the Manchester III. And so a major plank in Bomber Command's future operational structure was destined to come to fruition. In the meantime, Bomber Command would be saddled between 1941 and mid-1942 with what was regarded as an aerial "stinker"!

CHAPTER 1
Manchester Mk. I/IA

A rear view of the first prototype Manchester shows how a fairing occupies the location for the proposed rear turret. The rows of small windows, although an initial regular feature, would be blanked out on later-production airframes. Also revealed is the original 28-foot stabilizers, with large-mass balances for the elevators and the small-size fin/rudder structures. Still absent is the fixed, fabric-covered fin due to be located on the fuselage.

The original crew complement was set at six but would expand to seven in the light of the overall range of duties to be properly and efficiently carried out. There was a first and second pilot, but the second specialist was on hand only when needed. The other four were involved in the sharing of navigation, bomb aiming, wireless operation, and air gunnery. The increasing complexity involved in accurate navigation led to the splitting of this and the joint bomb-aiming duties enjoyed by what was known as the "Observer" into full-time "Navigator" and "Bomb Aimer" categories. Then the introduction of a dorsal turret to the existing duo of turrets led to the bomb aimer being tasked with manning the front turret, two of the now-specialist "Wireless Operator / Air Gunners" manning the remaining turrets and a third functioning permanently in the first-stated role.

The relatively small nature of prewar airfields with grass surfaces led to concerns about the ability of the range of modern bomber designs being able to get aloft in safe manner, a minimum of 50 feet on clearing the boundary being the criterion. In the case of the Manchester, the alternative of catapult launch was mooted. L7246 was accordingly dispatched to the Royal Aircraft Establishment (RAE) at Farnborough, where pictures exist of the airframe rigged up in the required manner, although no film or still-photo evidence confirms any degree of actual launch testing. In any event, none of the RAF's bombers were ever faced with operating in this manner, which would have required a mass of equipment as well as guaranteeing a greatly extended time span in getting an entire squadron airborne.

Tooling up at three factories (two Avro concerns and one of Metro-Vickers in and around Manchester) was completed and production begun in November 1939. The first production airframe, L7276, went to Boscombe Down for testing on handling; this was achieved with a 52,000-pound weight figure, although the all-up weight (AUW) limit had been set 5,000 pounds higher. Minor modifications to turrets and bomb bay notwithstanding, the overall performance was assessed as sound. L7277 was also fully tested while bearing an 8,000-pound bombload. An engine failure during one flight dictated that the maximum ceiling be reduced from 13,500 to 12,000 feet, still with a full load but with half the fuel capacity.

The original intention had the full production quota gone ahead was to equip at least twenty squadrons with the Avro bomber. In practice, barely a third of this figure (seven) was achieved, beginning with No. 207 Squadron in November 1940; the unit would operate the Manchester until January 1942, when the (surely thankful) conversion onto the Lancaster commenced. The first Manchester taken on was an airframe featuring an improvement in defensive armament in the form of the FN7 dorsal turret. However, the partial egg shape of the frame gave little comfort to the occupant; although a pair of doors at the rear provided a theoretical escape in an emergency, the chances of getting out through the minimal space ranged from poor to nonexistent.

More concerning for the entire crew was the continuing and unpredictable function of the Vulture, while faulty propeller-feathering controls along with hydraulic failures further added to the crews' sense of apprehension. As if this was not enough, an external danger arose from the start of Manchester operations in the form of *Nachtjagdgeschwader 2*; on March 13, L7319 EM:X was barely miles distant from Bottesford when a Ju 88 brought it down. Such was the dangerously inept performance of the Vulture that all aircraft were grounded in mid-April. "Friendly fire" incidents during World War II

The second prototype Manchester was L7247, which demonstrated the initial and only partially successful attempt to increase directional stability via the fin-and-rudder layout. The fixed "shark fin" central unit would give way to a larger unit; true stability would be achieved only on the Mk. IA, with twin fin-and-rudder structures of increased size compared to those on view here.

were rife, and after operations were resumed, L7314 EM:Y became the latest victim of a No. 25 Squadron Beaufighter on May 9. Ironically, the incident preceded a second grounding of the Manchester.

It was in mid-1941 that a major alteration to the fin and rudder occurred. The original three-fin structure applied to L7247 was regarded as no more than adequate in stability terms, with tail flutter and vibration regularly arising. In its place was fitted twin fin and rudder structures of greater size, along with an increase in stabilizer width from 28 to 33 feet that would be carried over to the Lancaster; the central fin was also deleted. This alteration merited a variant title change to Mk. IA, with L7489 the first airframe reconfigured.

Another key Vulture problem related to the failure of one engine, which reportedly increased the chances of a bomber failing to maintain level flight. A classic survival example involved a No. 207 crew in EM:Z/L7432, but it was only after jettisoning every excess item that the pilot (P/O "Kipper" Herring) managed to stagger back at minimum altitude when returning from Berlin! The regular incidence of engine failure even during nonoperational flight ended up with crews having to force-land in open countryside; thankfully the largely flat spaces of No. 5 Group's region of Lincolnshire ensured that most crews survived the experience, even if their already waning confidence in their mount was maintained! The Manchester's ability to successfully sustain heavy battle damage at least was attested to by official pictorial evidence, but the crews of No. 5 Group probably looked longingly to a more positive future with the introduction of an efficient successor. In March 1942, that hope began to be slowly realized when the first Lancasters commenced operations with Nos. 44 and 97 Squadrons, who duly stood down their Manchesters. By June, only Nos. 50, 61, 83, and 106 Squadrons were still Manchester equipped, but

changeover to the Lancaster was about to be made—an event that would introduce a quantum leap in Bomber Command's overall efficiency as a viable strike force.

The rear turret on the second Manchester prototype was of Frazer-Nash design. It was equipped with four .303-caliber machine guns and would become a standard feature on this Avro bomber. Along with twin-gun nose and dorsal turrets mounted on the Mk. IA, all provided from the same source, the arrangement would make for the heaviest armament borne by any British-produced twin-engine bomber serving with the RAF during World War II.

A lateral view of a No. 207 Squadron Manchester reveals the tail structure, which features the two smaller fin and rudders along with a fixed fin with no rudder on the fuselage. Also shown is the FN7 mid-upper turret and the large radio mast extending out of the main cockpit frame. L7319 was to become the victim of a *Luftwaffe* "Intruder" on March 13, 1942, having been operational with the unit for many months.

L7279 was a Mk. I Manchester assigned to No. 207 Squadron; this original variant bore the triple vertical fin stricture seen here. The airframe possesses the basic mounting for a ventral FN21A turret located directly behind the bomb bay, but very few if any airframes were actually equipped in this manner—a deficiency that would prove very costly from a point of view of challenging the *Nachtjagd* night fighters as they grew in operational efficiency.

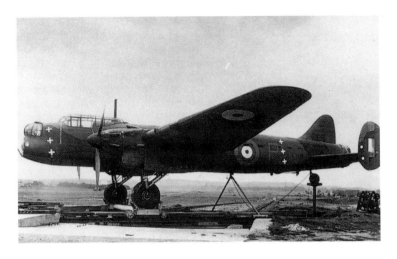

The average prewar RAF airfield's lack of runways and overall limited dimensions, which suited biplane operations up to the 1930s, was probably the reasons why catapult trials were initiated with the first prototype Manchester to ensure its safe airborne delivery in these circumstances. L7246 remained with the Royal Aircraft Establishment at Farnborough, where the tests were conducted but nothing practical emerged and the Manchester operated successfully in normal takeoff conditions.

The extended-length and single-cell nature of the Manchester bomb bay was greatly superior in load-carrying capacity to any of the three RAF heavy bombers at this point in World War II. The bombs seen on their trollies and ready for instalment within an anonymous Mk. I could be installed in greater quantity, while the open space allowed for the carriage of much-larger weapons such as the "Cookie," compared to the design's current contemporaries.

A view forward from the navigator's position shows the pilot and bomb aimer. The extension bar, bearing a second control column, is clearly depicted; in practice, the crew complement included just one pilot, however. Also note the folded-down armored headrest behind the pilot, the sole piece of such protection to be found either on the Manchester or Lancaster. The view from the overall cockpit frame was first class.

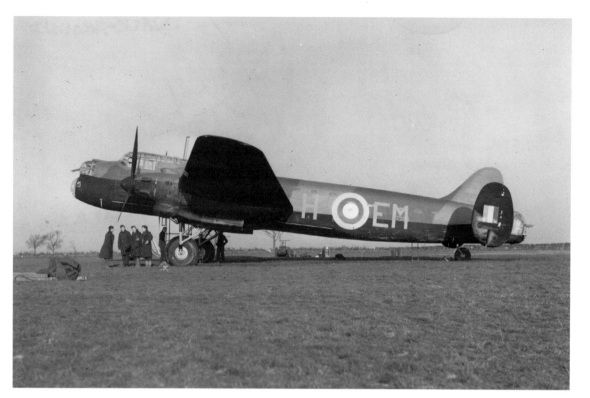

No. 207 Squadron was one of several within No. 5 Group to take on the Manchester in November 1940, having been reformed in the same month. The early airframes lacked the FN7 mid-upper turret, as seen here on L7288, photographed in September 1941—ironically a stage when the design's relegation from operational service was being actively pursued. The relatively small rudders on the outer fins, the central structure being fixed, provided a dangerously limited degree of control; replacement by larger structures that carried over onto the Lancaster proved necessary.

EM: D/L7284 is overflying the British countryside, with its often navigationally featureless terrain such as is depicted here. The fuselage camouflage split borne on a number of the original airframes would give way to the black portion being extended upward to leave a strip of the Dark Earth / Dark Green on the top surface. This aircraft transferred to No. 61 Squadron, and unlike many of its contemporaries it survived operations to be struck off charge (SOC) on June 18, 1943.

An anonymous Manchester possesses the changeover from the original three-fin structure to what would become the standard fitting on later-production Manchester Mk. IA airframes, as well as appearing on its Lancaster successor. The extended length of the rudders provided a greater measure of positive flight control for the pilot, as did the extension of the stabilizers from the original 28 feet to 33 feet. L7489 was the first to be modified on the production line, although in-the-field modifications were also made on then-operational Mk. I Manchester airframes.

An anonymous Manchester is photographed while undergoing an engine test, with the starboard Vulture engine's propeller, just in line with the front of the bomb bay, a visual blur. Ironically, the extremely inefficient performance of this engine type had emerged only in service, but the Manchester's development to four-engine status was already being considered during 1939. As matters transpired, the Vulture's displacement by its Rolls-Royce contemporary the Merlin on the Avro 683—whose Manchester Mk. III nomenclature would switch to Lancaster—was to prove the design's salvation.

Sgt. John Bushby (*left*) was the rear gunner on the No. 83 Squadron crew of W/O Whitehead (*right*). Bushby and Sgt. Dick Williams (next to Whitehead) were fated to be the known survivors from among the six crew members shown here, although they ended up as POWs in late 1942; the squadron by then was operating Lancasters within No. 8 (PFF) Group. The Welsh-language expression below the nocturnal insignia on the Manchester's nose translates to "All through the night."

Manchester L7515/EM:S was the tenth airframe to be modified to Mk. IA standard. It is being photographed from a Hampden for what is one of a series of publicity pictures. The amended camouflage split, with the Dark Earth / Dark Green top surface now limited to a relatively narrow strip terminating in a curve above the stabilizer leading edge, is clearly demonstrated. The No. 207 Squadron bomber served with three operational units and No. 1656 Conversion Unit (CU) before being SOC during November 1943.

The ever-present danger to Bomber Command aircraft and their crews striking into the heart of the Third Reich is demonstrated here on the fuselage of a No. 61 Squadron Manchester. The fuselage has absorbed punishment from flak that seems to have extended to the bomb bay doors, now detached for repair. The strikes were not sufficient to mortally damage the airframe; however, the proximity of the mid-upper FN7 turret to the impact point could have left its occupant in the path of the spray of lethal fragments, with serious or fatal injury effect.

The Manchester's rear turret was the Fraser-Nash (FN) 20, as seen on a triple-finned airframe. The rounded Plexiglas frame was subsequently displaced by a more vertical aligned frame marginally rounded at the top. The generously sized central panel afforded good visibility for the gunner but could become badly affected by poor weather conditions; the panel was initially modified to accommodate a rectangular sliding section, but some squadrons removed the entire central panel.

L7515 demonstrates the sound aerodynamic qualities of the Manchester airframe as the pilot banks steeply to starboard. The ability to carry out such a sharp maneuver even when fully loaded up for an operation would prove the future salvation of countless crews flying its Lancaster successor when intercepted by a *Nachtjagd* fighter; this of course was provided timely warning by the gunners in particular was transmitted to the pilot.

CHAPTER 2
Lancaster Mks. I and III

Dimensions	
Wingspan	102 ft.
Length	69 ft. 6 in.
Height	20 ft. 6 in.
Wing area	1,297 sq. ft.
Tailplane area	237 sq. ft.

Performance	
Maximum speed	ranging from 287 mph at 11,000 ft. to 260 mph at 19,400 ft.
Cruising speed	from 234 mph at 21,000 ft. to 200 mph at 15,000 ft.
Stalling speed	95 mph
Service ceiling	23,000 ft.
Absolute ceiling	24,000 ft.
Climb rate	250 ft./min.

Range
2,530 miles with a 7,000-lb. bombload
1,730 miles with a 12,000-lb. bombload
1,550 miles with a 22,000-lb. bombload

(this latter calculation was surely not made at the outset of the Lancaster's career, since the figure would equate with the "Grand Slam" aerodynamic weapon, which did not come into consideration until well on into World War II).

The transformation from relative failure to success for the Avro design was proposed to the Air Ministry by Roy Chadwick; his confidence that a "phoenix from the ashes" scenario would evolve was supported by the air member for development and production, Air Marshal Sir Wilfred Freeman; an ironic twist in the latter's stance was that he had stated in a letter dated July 29, 1940, that Avro was to be ordered to produce the four-engine Handley-Page Halifax as opposed to proceeding with the Avro 683, which was at this point titled the Manchester Mk. III. A swift visit by Chadwick to Freeman was equally swiftly followed by a joint discussion with the Ministry of Aircraft Production's (MAP) senior staff, which resulted in a resurrection of the Avro 683's development.

The prototype airframe BT308 was on hand by December 1940, with an overall outline that would became standard albeit with one exception; this related to the triple-fin layout applied to the original batch of Manchesters. Enlarged twin fin/rudder structures were due to be introduced on the prototype, along with the center fin's deletion. Nevertheless, it would be well over a month following BT308 first going aloft on January 4, 1941, before this necessary conversion would take place.

The Lancaster's fuel capacity, which remained a standard feature on the aircraft, was 2,154 gallons split between three tanks in either wing. Overload tanks could be accommodated in the bomb bay but were never a regular aspect of operational function. The all-up weight (AUW) would witness a steady increase from the 60,000-pound limit applying to the early Mk. I as well as the Mk. II, advancing to 63,000 pounds on later-production Mk. Is during 1942, and then 65,000 pounds on 1944 production Mks. I and III. The AUW peak would be attained on 1945-produced Mk. I and III airframes tasked with overload capability, a 72,000-pound figure being set.

These statistics were a quantum leap in operational efficiency, even compared to the bomber designs with which the RAF had entered the conflict, and spelled serious trouble for the Third Reich's industrial capability. A further indication of operational efficiency was the ability of the Lancaster to remain aloft even when down to single-engine function, although a steady loss of altitude was experienced in this instance.

The second prototype, DG595, was airborne during April, and the handling trials of both progressed positively, with the aircraft heading to Boscombe Down, home for the Aircraft and Armament Experimental Establishment (A. and A.E.E.) during August. By then, the first production contract had been officially issued for 454 airframes, this being the precursor for an ultimate production figure of 7,377 to emerge during and after World War II. The tests indicated that elevator and aileron control responded well at either end of a 100–290 mph range, but pressure on the rudders built up as speed increased. A distinct tendency to swing to port during takeoff was countered by opening the port outer engine throttle and lifting the tail up as quickly as possible to get the rudders in play, this twin action counteracting what was the effect of torque caused by propeller rotation to starboard. A marginal wingspan increase from 100 to 102 feet was carried out on the production lines after weakness in the wingtips was discovered during testing; the alteration also resulted in retrospective amendment of the Lancasters already in service with No. 44 Squadron.

The Merlin X, rated at 1,145 hp, had been fitted to BT308 if not also DG595, but production airframes would see a switch to the Merlin XX, whose rating was enhanced by 150 hp, as well as the Merlin 22, of similar power output, and later the Merlin V24, with a much-greater 1,620 hp capability. The variable-pitch three-blade propellers were De Havilland 5/40s but were to prove interchangeable with the Hamilton A5/138 equivalent unit. The need for such a potentially massive production scale to be accommodated by a manufacturing group was recognized by the linking of Avro with the Armstrong-Whitworth, Metropolitan-Vickers, Austin Motors, and Vickers-Armstrong concerns.

The pressure on Britain's industrial capacity was ever critical; coupled with the assaults of the *Luftwaffe* was added the even more insidious U-boat attacks on the convoy system, which further ate into the material resources with which to maintain satisfactory levels of production. The prospect of Merlin engine output falling below levels needed to keep the Lancaster squadrons viably operational led to the proposal that a secondary production source be sought. In this case the Bristol Company's Hercules radial engine, regarded as a suitable alternative, was chosen and fitted to airframes DT810 and 812; the former went airborne in November 1941, to become the prototype for 300 aircraft destined to be constructed by the Armstrong-Whitworth Company (the Packard Company would also build Merlins under subcontract that would power the Mk. I/III as well as the Canadian-produced Mk. X).

The arrival of the Lancaster into RAF service came at a very critical time for Bomber Command. The late-1941 Butt Report, detailing the severe limitations on target location and therefore even basic bombing accuracy achieved to date, had placed Bomber

BT308 was the first Lancaster prototype but still retained the original Manchester fin-and-rudder structure, rear turret, and fixed radio mast. The wingspan has been lengthened from 90 to 100 feet, and four Merlins have replaced the two Rolls-Royce Vultures, which had proved so dangerously ineffective in overall performance.

Command squarely on its back foot, perhaps to the extent of querying its very existence as a viable element in striking effectively at Nazi Germany. The virtually parallel arrival as commander in chief ("C-in-C") of Air Chief Marshal (ACM) Arthur "Bomber" Harris did not immediately guarantee a swift change in the bombing offensive's fortunes, and it would be well into 1942 before this would thankfully first arise; the Lancaster would prove a key albeit still-limited element in effecting this advance toward hammering the enemy's industrial base.

By 1942, the crew complement on the Lancaster and Halifax had been standardized at seven, albeit with a functional crew change; in place of a second pilot, a flight engineer was introduced. His primary duty was to monitor the engine and fuel systems and assist the pilot with the throttles during takeoff and landing.

BT308 is seen overflying the main production plant's airfield. The Manchester Mk. IA's later-pattern fin-and-rudder layout is in place, but the fixed radio mast remains while defensive armament is limited to the nose and rear turrets. The underwing type A roundels would be dispensed with on production bombers.

DG585 is fully modified to future Lancaster format, with BT308's 100-foot wingspan being extended to the standard 102 feet. The radio mast has given way to aerial cables extending from the cockpit frame to the upper-fin leading edges. The reframed FN20 unit and a FN50 mid-upper turret will become standard units. A yellow "P" in a circle denotes a prototype airframe. The Dark Earth / Dark Green upper camouflage blends well with the countryside.

The British public was made aware of the Lancaster's existence only during mid-1942, several months after active operations commenced around March 1942. VN:N/R5689, assigned to No. 50 Squadron, was the chosen example, and the photo sequence was taken on August 28. Less than one month later the bomber lost partial power during landing approach off a mine-laying operation and crashed, a failure that caused some crew fatalities.

A detailed view of a Lancaster under assembly picks out the flexible panel forming the wing leading edge, which permits access to the cables running along the main spar's facing. The framework for the inboard Merlin engine nacelle is also depicted. This is an early-production bomber as confirmed by the FN50 turret, which lacks the tracking frame at its base, which prevented the gunner from inadvertently firing into the airframe.

A closer examination of the Lancaster's rear fuselage section picks out the raised cover surrounding the mid-upper turret base. Inside is the tracking frame that elevates the guns clear of the airframe. The rectangular aperture just ahead of the rear turret and its equivalent on the starboard side provide access for the stabilizer main frame. ND824 joined No. 83 Squadron in April 1944 and survived operation to be finally SOC in November 1946.

One Lancaster, ready to roll out of the production factory; with just the upper nacelle panels to be put in place once each engine has been test run, the majestic Avro bomber is being towed. The light strips on the fuselage and wings indicate the section joins, which was now covered by masking tape.

Initial Operations

Nocturnal operations would almost exclusively be the norm for Bomber Command's crews until around D-day. In the Lancaster's case, the inaugural operation was not against a land target. Instead, on March 3–4, four crews from No. 44 Squadron laid sea mines; No. 97 Squadron's debut on the twentieth involved the same function, although the sortie to the Frisian Island chain was, unusually, conducted during daylight hours. A mine-laying run to Lorient five nights later saw the first of 3,347 Lancasters fated to go missing in action (MIA) during World War II, when the former-listed unit's KM:M/R5493 went down.

The presence of six ground crew members in this picture is a clear indication it is a publicity-oriented shot, since the standard teams did not comprise this number. The Rolls-Royce Merlin was a superbly efficient power plant both for the RAF and, in particular, the USAAF's P-51B and D escort fighters, with the latter design a key factor in breaking the back of the *Jagdwaffe* during early 1944.

Armament

The standard armament on a Mk. I or III initially comprised four turrets, but the FN64 ventral unit was deleted early on. The upper nose FN5 and the mid-upper FN50 each carried two .303-caliber machine guns, while the FN20 rear turret doubled up on this figure. On initial production airframes, the mid-upper turret's unrestricted movement in azimuth and elevation raised a clear risk of the gunner inadvertently firing into the airframe should the guns be depressed too low. A tracking device was accordingly introduced that elevated the weapons in order to avoid the risk, with the cockpit and fins specially in mind, and this was enclosed in a contoured fairing.

One signal weakness that was never more than marginally addressed during the conflict was the RAF's reliance on the .303-caliber bullet, particularly as a defensive means on its bombers. The range and striking power afforded by the ammunition was greatly outweighed by the 13 mm bullet and 20 mm cannon-caliber weapons in mass use by the German fighters. In the case of the Lancaster this often-lethal imbalance was soon brought to bear on April 17, 1942. The two current squadrons were tasked with attacking the MAN factory at Augsburg, deep in southeastern Germany—and by day at that. The six-strong force from No. 44 Squadron unfortunately ran into *Luftwaffe* Fw 190s returning from challenging a diversion by RAF fighters. In the ensuing air battle, no fewer than four Lancasters were clinically dispatched, with their eight machine guns, split between the three turrets, being simply overwhelmed by the weight of counter gunfire. Three further crews were lost before the raid was over, and the award of the Victoria Cross to S/Ldr. Nettleton (44 Squadron) was little consolation even if a sizable though temporary scale of destruction was visited upon the target.

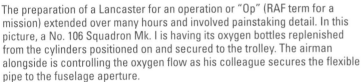

The preparation of a Lancaster for an operation or "Op" (RAF term for a mission) extended over many hours and involved painstaking detail. In this picture, a No. 106 Squadron Mk. I is having its oxygen bottles replenished from the cylinders positioned on and secured to the trolley. The airman alongside is controlling the oxygen flow as his colleague secures the flexible pipe to the fuselage aperture.

The four-gun complement for the FN20 rear turret is being placed in position. The .303-caliber weaponry that was favored by the RAF authorities was barely adequate in striking power compared to the largely cannon-caliber equivalent in *Luftwaffe* use; the latter form of armament also enjoyed a greater range capability—so the operationally seasoned RAF gunner desisted from engaging an adversary unless absolutely impelled to do so!

The Rose-Rice Company had manufactured a turret that employed twin .50-caliber machine guns. The enlarged frame enabled the gunner to bear his parachute on his harness, while the low-slung nature of the gun-mounting frame and the open-ended turret front permitted him the opportunity to bail out directly as opposed to seeking his pack from within the fuselage before doing so. Equally important was the greater striking power of the .50-caliber bullet, which, as the USAAF experience proved, had an effect on an airframe nearly as deadly as that of a cannon-caliber weapon but also permitted an ammunition load capacity nearer to that of the .303-caliber and far ahead of the cannon's equivalent total. Sadly, the turret was introduced only late in World War II, as well as in limited numbers.

The quartet of cylindrical shapes resting on trolleys forms the primary bomb in regular Bomber Command usage during World War II. Known as the "Cookie," the 90/10 percent ratio of the weapon's explosive to case weight ensured a maximum blast effect on the target structures. The Lancasters usually carried a single example as the centerpiece of a bombload. Although the Lancaster bears No. 83 Squadron codes, these only partially conceal the KM codes for the aircraft's originally assigned unit (No. 44 Squadron).

Another caliber of bomb in large-scale operational use weighed in at 1,000 pounds. The carrier frame is being attached to the weapon via twin sets of clamps. The frame's lifting cable is also attached, and the entire assembly will be raised into the bomb bay by using a portable hand-crank unit. The picture was taken at Syerston, the base for No. 106 Squadron in 1942–43, whose CO was W/Comm. Guy Gibson, future leader for No. 617 "Dambusters" Squadron.

The final stage of operational readiness has been achieved for an anonymous Lancaster. Now, the black-clad personnel relax around the dispersal point as the four Merlins are opened up to full pitch, with the propeller blades almost disappearing from sight. Everything possible has been done to ensure a maximum state of technical security for the seven aircrew destined to take their charge into battle.

Pilot Sgt. John Mackintosh (*center*) and his flight engineer Sgt. Ron Sooley (*right*) of No. 207 Squadron prepare for start-up. This duo of crew members on a Lancaster were the only ones out of the seven-man team functioning alongside each other. Sooley's control panel is on the starboard side of the cockpit; his function is primarily to monitor engine performance and fuel flow. Sgt. Ian Hutchison (navigator) appears in the left foreground; his lack of a helmet suggests this is a publicity shot.

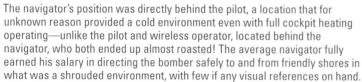

The navigator's position was directly behind the pilot, a location that for unknown reason provided a cold environment even with full cockpit heating operating—unlike the pilot and wireless operator, located behind the navigator, who both ended up almost roasted! The average navigator fully earned his salary in directing the bomber safely to and from friendly shores in what was a shrouded environment, with few if any visual references on hand.

The bomb aimer occupied the forward compartment. Sgt. Desmond Ball was part of the No. 207 Squadron crew headed by Sgt. John Mackintosh and is seen studying a map, possibly with a view to assisting the navigator by seeking out geographic pinpoints. Ball was one of two crew members who survived his tour with No. 207 Squadron, only to go MIA during his second operational tour.

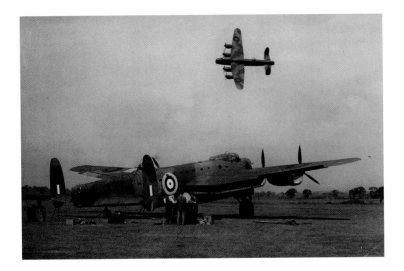

The Lancaster banking to port and displaying the top camouflage pattern is bypassing DG585, the second prototype airframe. Points of note on the latter are the FN64 ventral gun turret, seen visually in line with the starboard fin/rudder and the astrodome on the forward cockpit frame, which was dispensed with on the production line. Aircraft also appears to have the FN50 "taboo track" in place. Degaussing cable lengths surround the fuselage at this point, although the censor's reference ironically highlights the fact.

A Lancaster serving with No. 101 Sqdn. is snapped just as the bomb aimer has pressed the release button, and the bomb bay is disgorging the single "Cookie" along with a rain of incendiaries. This combination of explosive and fire-raising weapons was dubbed "Usual" and was the basic load employed by Bomber Command during the campaign from 1942 onward.

Automatic Gun-Laying Turret (AGLT)

Between May 1940 and the late summer of 1944, the air gunners within Bomber Command were dependent on visual acuity when scanning the nocturnal skies for enemy fighters. This was a constant physical and, arguably, also a psychological strain on these airmen as they sought to bring themselves and their crew colleagues safely through an operation. However, electronic means were finally on hand with which to confirm the presence of and automatically engage an encroaching *Nachtjagd* fighter—provided the approach was being initiated from the rear. As it was, the vast bulk of assaults would be launched from this direction during the offensive, a measure that suited the equipment granted the nomenclature title of Automatic Gun-Laying Turret (AGLT) and code-named Village Inn.

The device was housed in a tubular cover positioned below the rear turret. The gunner was made aware of a bogey closing in by means of an aural signal that increased in frequency; when within range, the gunner engaged the target source. The obvious problem lay in identifying the bogey as a hostile as opposed to a friendly aircraft, in similar manner to the "Monica" tail-warning equipment. However, unlike "Monica," the solution was to mount twin receivers that in the case of the Lancaster were housed in circular mounts positioned centrally on the bomb aimer's Plexiglas bubble; these would be picked up by the AGLT equipment and give the gunner a positive indication—something absent from a similar approach by a *Luftwaffe* aircraft.

Two squadrons, Nos. 49 and 189, based at Fiskerton and Fulbeck in late 1944, were chosen to have the equipment installed, after which the first operational use was indulged in. F/Lt. Will Hay's bomber, bearing the author's uncle as bomb aimer, gave an account of the operation; the squadron was allocated the rearmost position in the No. 5 Group bomber stream in order to provide the maximum chance of engaging a night fighter, and conversely avoiding all contact with friendly aircraft—a situation that naturally left the AGLT force dangerously exposed.

Suddenly, F/Lt. John Hall, at the back, picked up signals that finally evolved into not one but three Ju 88s, and the fight was on. It was obviously fortunate that the enemy pilots did not coordinate their passes in order to divide Hall's and Sgt. French's dorsal turrets' return fire; in any event, EA:G/PB354 survived with no material damage, by which stage just one machine gun in Hall's complement of four was still functioning! The operational experiment appears to have been confined to the two squadrons and did not result in a wholesale distribution of the AGLT system throughout Bomber Command before the conclusion of the offensive.

The wireless operator, known as "Sparks" from the pattern on his uniform arm patch, worked with the transmitter/receiver (TR) set attached to the bulkhead. His right hand covers the Morse code key. His duty was mostly passive, listening for any messages in practice. The presence of the warm-air outlet alongside him ensured extreme discomfort when full heating was applied!

The mid-upper turret formed the defensive means of combating fighter attacks from a level or high angle. The FN50's minimal amount of framework ensured that the gunner had a good overall field of vision. Unfortunately, the bulk of nocturnal assaults was delivered from lower down, so the gunner's ability to add to the rear gunner's efforts was rather limited. In addition, entry into and, even more critically, exit from the position in an emergency were none too easy.

Sgt. Roland Middleton, on Sgt. Mackintosh's No. 207 Squadron bomber, is seen entering his rear turret position. An inability to take the parachute pack inside due to lack of space forced the occupant to exit and then collect his pack from a nearby rack before attempting to jump—all right if time allowed, but difficult if not impossible to achieve if the aircraft was going out of control. Middleton suffered the same fate as Sgt. Ball (MIA) while he too was flying a second operational tour.

The faded-light conditions form a dramatic backdrop for four Lancasters belonging to No. 49 Squadron as they squat on their dispersals at Scampton. The airfield was one of the permanent structures introduced during the late 1930s, with five type C or D hangars and brick support buildings. At this stage of World War II (1942–43), the airfield surface other than the metal-surface dispersals was grass covered.

Ops are on, and a line of Lancasters from No. 83 Squadron—operating from Scampton until transfer to No. 8 (PFF) Group in August 1942—is lined up in an arc and ready for takeoff. The F/Lt. with the Aldis lamp has granted clearance for takeoff to the bomber in the foreground, which has probably already commenced its run; the grassy nature of the airfield surface is more evident in this picture. Concrete runway replacements would not occur until the latter half of 1943.

"The Heart of War" is absorbing the force dispatched to Hamburg on January 31, 1943. The single Lancaster tracking along the bomb run at a torturously steady rate while outlined against a confusing miasma of flares, flak bursts, and bomb detonations is dangerously exposed to further interception by night fighters. These would sometimes intrude even over the target area, despite the inherent danger of being struck by "friendly fire."

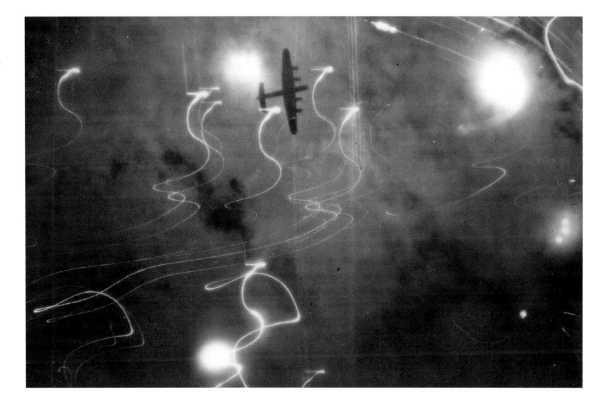

An Op's overall duration could extend up to ten hours—that is, for those crews fortunate enough to run the gauntlet of fighters and flak. In this grimly beautiful picture, a No. 106 Squadron bomber's outline is heightened by the moonlight reflecting off the clouds. The aircraft, which is an early-production machine according to the mid-upper turret's lack of a frame surround to its base, is taxiing toward its dispersal with the outboard engines switched off.

The clearance of snow from a bomber's surfaces was a tedious but absolutely vital task; the danger of ice-accretion adversely affecting the control surfaces—whether on take-off or when flying at altitude—was the primary reason for the activity. Working high above the ground on the ever-slippery wing surfaces with their sharp camber presented the risk of injury or even death should an airman lose his footing.

DV372 joined No. 467 Squadron at Waddington in November 1943 and survived operations for one year before assignment to No. 1651 Conversion Unit (CU). Here the noncommissioned officer (NCO) (*second from right*) in charge of the ground crew is taking notes from the pilot (*fourth from right*). Once completed, all seven airmen will be transported to the debriefing room. This picture was probably taken during the 1943–44 winter campaign, when Berlin formed the epicenter of the nocturnal assault on Germany.

Evacuation

The interior of any World War II multicrew design was such that swift movement from one point to another was slow in normal flight; movement in an emergency was even more constrained, given the need to gain access to the various escape hatches, but this was made doubly critical should the aircraft begin to go, or already be, out of control. Fire, especially within the fuselage, was an even-greater impediment to speedy and safe exit. The pilot on a Lancaster was the only member with a seat-pack parachute, his crew having to rely on gaining access to and clipping on their packs to the flight harness clips. The four members up front evacuated via the hatch positioned in the bomb aimer's compartment; however, the radio operator's position, being behind the bulky wing main spar, made the entrance hatch a better choice for him.

An extra escape route existed within the cockpit roof in the form of a detachable section above the pilot's seat, but its use posed several risks; the mid-upper turret, directly in line, could be a lethal obstacle if it was accidentally bumped, while the twin aerial wires would literally act as a guillotine should the slipstream impel the individual's body off to one side and into their path.

Arguably most constrained in this manner were the gunners; the mid-upper gunner had to clamber down from his position, grab his pack attached to the fuselage, and make for the entrance door. The tail gunner's experience was even more fraught; he had to get back into the rear fuselage to get his pack, regain the turret, swivel it around, and flip himself out backward—all this, provided the turret hydraulics still functioned. Of course he could follow his companion out via the entrance door. Both would also have to ensure that they made a low exit in order to avoid contact with the horizontal stabilizer.

In these circumstances, it is none too surprising that the percentage of bomber crews failing either individually or sometimes in total to escape alive from what now amounted to an aerial tomb was frighteningly high. The Lancaster was no exception to this feral situation and indeed proved to be the most lethal among the trio of four-engine heavies prosecuting the bombing offensive.

Closer view of the mid-upper turret on a crash-landed No. 106 Squadron "Lanc" picks out the projections at the base of the gun apertures. These were part of the tracking device concealed under the turret fairing, which prevented accidental depression of the weapons to a degree where they were in line with the airframe. Circular vents on the turret top allow the guns' cordite fumes to escape. The compartment on the inner starboard wing normally houses the crew's inflatable dinghy.

The shattered Plexiglas panel and turret frame liberally peppered with shell or bullet strikes bears sad witness to No. 57 Squadron's Sgt. P. Hayes's fate in ED413/DX:M on June 15, 1943, during a raid over Oberhausen. The striking power of the four .303-caliber machine guns was nothing as effective as that delivered by the *Nachtjagd* cannon-equipped fighters There was little security from injury or death for any bomber crew member, but the rear gunners were particularly prone to suffering either fate compared to their colleagues.

A flight of three Lancasters from No. 207 Squadron present a tight formation against a skyline formed of broken cumulonimbus clouds. The code letters on EM:C and EM:A are smaller in scale compared to their companion bomber. This picture was shot after June 1942, when the type A1 fuselage roundels and fin flashes gave way to the less visible type C1 design on all RAF aircraft. Daylight formations of this nature would occur only around and beyond D-day, when the Bomber Command could more safely operate with *Luftwaffe* resources, critically limited due to Allied aerial superiority.

The Lancaster's fuel capacity was 2,154 gallons, contained in six wing tanks. Here the main standard RAF vehicle, an AEC Matador with a capacity of 2,600 gallons, has part of its load delivered to the port inner tank. The row of small bomb containers (SBCs) will hold over 200 4-pound incendiary weapons. The SBCs, along with the 4,000-pound "Cookie," formed a sizable proportion of the total tonnage dropped by Bomber Command during World War II.

A train of four trolleys, each bearing a medium-capacity (MC) bomb, is lined up in front of a Lancaster's brooding outline, ready for positioning under the Avro bomber's massive 33-foot-long bomb bay. The large number of ground crew on hand indicates that this is a publicity photo. The needle-bladed propellers originally applied to the design later gave way to paddle blades, which provided an enhanced performance in climb rate, for example.

W4117 was typical of operationally tested Lancasters that were subsequently assigned to advanced training units such as Heavy Conversion Units (HCUs) or Lancaster Finishing Schools (LFS). The bomber had served with Nos. 49 and 156 (PFF) Squadrons prior to reassignment. The GP code letters refer to No. 1661 HCU, based at Winthorpe from January 1943 onward. Later service with No. 5 LFS followed.

The loading of a No. 83 Squadron bomber is complete with what was christened a "usual" load. This consisted of a single "Cookie" surrounded by twelve SBC units. The effect arising from the "Cookie's" detonation within the blast zone was expected to prepare the way for the myriad of incendiary bombs released from the SBCs to infiltrate the fractured surfaces of buildings and set them alight. This was "Total War" in one of its most brutal formats, albeit inevitable in the circumstances when given the visual constraints of nocturnal operations.

A variation in bombload content is displayed on this dispersal, believed to be at Mepal, home for No. 75 (New Zealand) Squadron. The SBC element is restricted to eight units, while four 1,000-pound bombs take the place of the missing incendiary containers. The "Cookie" still forms the core of the load. The Lancaster's 33-foot, single-cell bomb bay could accommodate up to 18,000 pounds of weaponry.

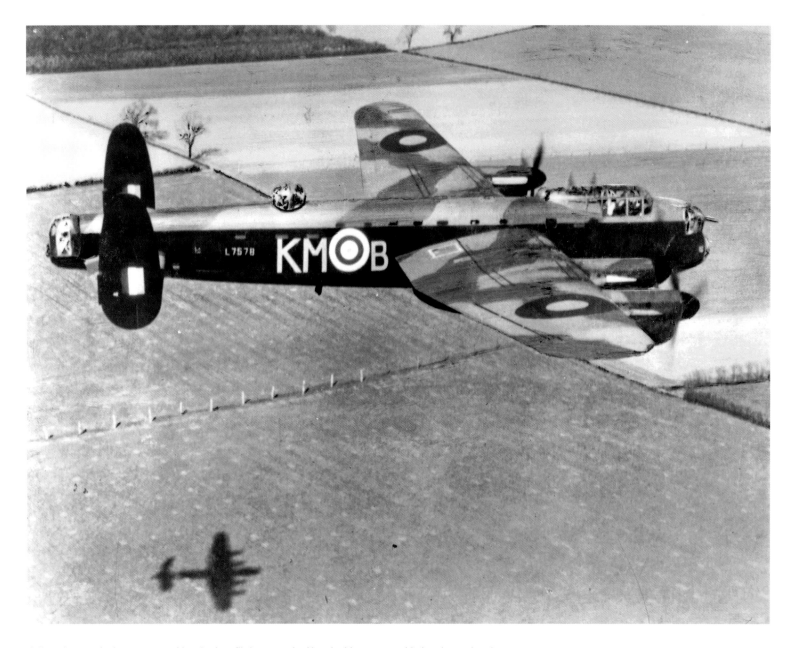

A fine picture of a Lancaster and its shadow flitting over the Lincolnshire countryside involves a bomber bearing No. 44 Squadron codes. On April 17, 1942, twelve crews from this and No. 97 Squadron carried out a daring long-range daylight operation to bomb the MAN plant at Augsburg in southeast Germany, which produced U-boat diesel engines. The stub fitting below the letter "M" is the sheath for the trailing aerial. Aircraft here actually belonged to No. 97 despite the code letter confusion!

The RAF heavy bombers never possessed the equivalent of the USAAF's ball turret, although early examples featured the FN64 mounting, with twin guns, and some carried a single gun in a manual mount. The photo angle demonstrates the vulnerability of the RAF heavies to night-fighter approach *von hinten, unten* ("from behind and below" in German). They were even more exposed to the *Schräge Musik* ("jazz music"), the nickname for the upward-firing cannon introduced from mid-1943 onward that consumed hundreds of aircraft, along with many of their crews.

Bombload

Any conflict, especially one conducted on the scale and pace of World War II, demanded swift advances in the technological means with which to achieve, it was hoped, an ultimate victory. The bombing offensive was a key example of this factor. In 1939, the RAF bombs in use were generally extremely small in size and accordingly ineffectual in their destructive capability; the 500-pound bomb on hand was regarded as representing the upper limits needed to achieve a good strike effect, while the 250-pound bomb was available in even-greater quantity. This was a sad reflection on such offensive weaponry's marginal prospects of effectively eliminating any target, whether industrial or military in nature.

By 1940–41, the Air Ministry had woken up to the limitations of the range of bombs on hand. The "area" nature of the nocturnal campaign had witnessed the introduction first of 1,000-pound and even 2,000-pound designs; in addition, the need for armor-piercing examples with which to penetrate more-solid structures had been realized. However, the largest bomb type to date totally reversed the trend toward streamlining, in the form of the 4,000-pound "Cookie," introduced during 1941.

The parallel-sided cylindrical shape was bereft of any tail fins and was a thin-skinned unit with a case-weight/explosive ratio of 10/90 percent. Its release in conjunction with a mass of

Crash-landing any aircraft is a risky business, as this Lancaster demonstrates. The aircraft's momentum was thankfully spent before it made what would have been contact with the railway line as well as several telegraph poles. The impressive bomb log, totaling around seventy symbols, attests to this example as a true operational survivor, but the scale of damage, which seems to include separation of most of the port wing, indicates it will never again fly on operations, if indeed at all.

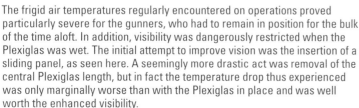

The frigid air temperatures regularly encountered on operations proved particularly severe for the gunners, who had to remain in position for the bulk of the time aloft. In addition, visibility was dangerously restricted when the Plexiglas was wet. The initial attempt to improve vision was the insertion of a sliding panel, as seen here. A seemingly more drastic act was removal of the central Plexiglas length, but in fact the temperature drop thus experienced was only marginally worse than with the Plexiglas in place and was well worth the enhanced visibility.

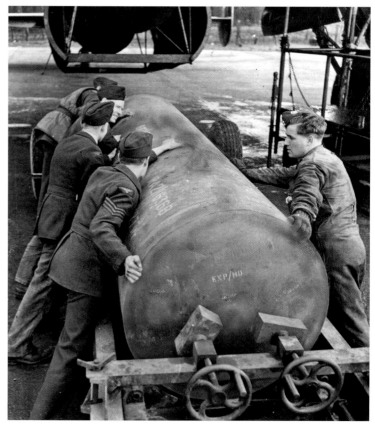

The party of ground crew is pushing what looks like a massive boiler but is in fact an 8,000-pound variant of the "Cookie." Of equal interest are the bomb bay doors on a No. 106 Squadron bomber. These are wooden instead of metal, are held open by a frame, and moreover have no hydraulic system for deployment. Instead the weight of the bomb released on the surfaces would cause them to spring open. This picture was taken at Syerston, where the squadron was then based.

incendiaries was intended to create a blast effect on buildings, the incendiaries gaining access to the interior through the gaps rent by the explosive force of the "Cookie." This was to be a principal operational aspect of Bomber Command operations from late 1941 onward that in turn reflected the cruder elements of what was sadly a Total War scenario—area bombing—forced on the RAF due to a then-current inability to operate effectively by day without incurring unsustainable loss rates in bombers and crews.

The Lancaster's inheritance of the 33-foot, single-cell bomb bay introduced on the Manchester added to its overall effective performance. Within this massive space could be accommodated up to 18,000 pounds of bombs and incendiaries; in practice, the

maximum loads varied between 10,000 and 14,000 pounds, but even so, these figures were well ahead of its Halifax and Stirling contemporaries. The equivalent maximum internally stowed figures for the B-17 (6,000 pounds) and B-24 (8,000 pounds) seem even more of a disparity; however, the need for a crew walkway in the middle of each USAAF bomber's bomb bay caused a lateral restriction on the maximum size of bombs capable of being stowed (2,000 pounds). The real irony lies in the fact that the USAAF could potentially achieve much more accurate strikes, but at an appreciably reduced individual load compared to the RAF; the latter in turn suffered a serious degradation in accurate bombing during nocturnal operations, albeit with a reverse ability to deliver much-heavier individual loads.

RAF aircraft featured in numerous national fund-raising exercises during the conflict. L7580 was the centerpiece for this display held in London's Trafalgar Square. "O" for Orange had put in thirteen Ops at this point in its operational career, according to the placard, and moreover bucked the trend for survival rates (estimated at no more than eleven operations for the average bomber) by still being on hand at the conclusion of hostilities.

Ludford Magna was the No. 1 Group base for No. 101 Squadron and its Lancasters. This is ED382, one of 129 Mk. I airframes out of a total batch of 620, the remainder receiving Packard Merlins and designated as Mk. III, compared to the Rolls-Royce engines mounted in the Mk. I. The heavy exhaust staining is especially evident on the inboard engines of this and the bomber in the background. Absence of staining on the rear wing section behind the no. 1 engine indicates it is a replacement. ED382 survived operations with this and two subsequent squadrons.

Mk. III Lancaster

The Rolls-Royce Merlin was to prove one of the most efficient power plants to be applied to RAF aircraft. The success of the Spitfire, Hurricane, and Mosquito designs along with the Lancaster amply proved that point during World War II; it is safe to say that the operational superiority of all four aircraft owed almost as much to this factor as to their aerodynamic qualities. In contrast to this positive factor was set a likely logistical limitation; namely, the threat that the UK's manufacturing ability could be placed under inordinate pressure to the extent of not being able to sustain the production flow on Merlins, for instance. The 1942 output target, set at around 18,000, although substantial, was still regarded as no more than adequate.

The ultimate switch to the Bristol Hercules was a point in case, and a similar situation culminated in an alternative production source for the Merlin; however, the location for the latter power plant lay not within the United Kingdom but across the Atlantic in the United States. The Packard Company was offered and agreed to a contract for regular production, but in fact the Ford Company had already been in possession of the blueprints since mid-1940. Not only did this boost to production guarantee a continued flow of Merlins; the US environment, being immune from any form of aerial assault, meant that production remained free of any such potentially serious constraint.

The Packard variation was designated Merlin 28, and preproduction examples had been air-tested using two Lancasters during 1942. The American power plant involved some variations vis-à-vis its Rolls-Royce twin, with the carburetor system a key example; the Bendix Stromberg unit employed a pressure injection function for the fuel similar to that in *Luftwaffe* use. A tendency to overheat should regular takeoffs and landings be the norm—a feature of Heavy Conversion Unit and Lancaster Finishing School training-unit activity—witnessed the use of the Mk. I in this role; otherwise, the Packard Merlin performed equally well operationally. Also, the tolerances on machined parts were reportedly of a finer nature than with Rolls-Royce units. There was also a feature that held the RAF ground crews' attention; namely, the provision of a far more comprehensive set of tools with each engine than was the case with the parsimonious attitude to such a basic detail existing within Air Ministry supply circles!

As the Packard engines built up in numbers, so their importation and allocation to the factory line production of Lancasters during mid-1943 witnessed a designation change to airframes so equipped. This took the form of a Mk. III nomenclature for the bombers so outfitted. In practice there was no discernible external difference between a Mk. I and a Mk. III airframe; only the individual serial number would confirm to which variation the airframe belonged. Indeed, there were instances where a Lancaster operated both with Rolls-Royce- and Packard-produced engines, although the ground crew concerned would naturally have to possess technical familiarity with both subtypes.

Flaps are set at 30 degrees and the radiator shutters are open as the pilot of PA170/LS:N prepares to advance the throttles and trundle down the runway at Mildenhall. The intended daylight raid on Essen occurred during the bomber's relatively short operational spell with the squadron between October and December 4, 1944, when it was MIA, becoming the sole loss from 160 within the No. 3 Group force.

No. 514 Sqdn. took on the Mk. II Lancaster in September 1943 but converted onto the Mk. I and III the following July. LM181/JI:E came from the former subrank that operated on the Rolls-Royce Merlin. The bomber was fated to be lost along with its entire crew, one of four squadron losses; these in turn formed 20 percent of No. 3 Group's casualty list over the synthetic oil pant at Homburg, Germany, on July 20–21, 1944.

The metal containers hold homing pigeons; these would be released, for example, once a ditched crew had clambered into their dinghy with the coordinates of the incident position written down and placed in a metal tube attached to the bird's leg. The heavily lined yellow flight suit borne by man on the left indicates he is one of the gunners, whose positions were particularly bereft of any heat control source. Note the variation in footwear on the right-hand man.

The Lancaster's sturdy airframe could accommodate a degree of damage that was seemingly lethal, and still remain airborne. On October 21, 1943, P/O Britton's bomber sustained severe flak or fighter gunfire that among other strikes reduced the starboard fin and rudder to this perilous state. The pilot still retained overall control and landed safely back in Britain. The squadron concerned is unknown to the author.

This picture of a Mk. I Lancaster was taken at Syerston during the latter half of 1942. The cylindrical objects on the trolleys are parachute-assisted sea mines ready for loading into one of No. 106 Squadron's bombers. Unit conversion from the dangerously inefficient Manchester is unconsciously confirmed by the presence in the left background of one of the twin-engine airframes with its distinctive trio of fins. Several Lancasters bore artwork, with the wording having the prefix "Admiral," a throwback from the CO's (W/ Comm. Guy Gibson) former service with No. 83 Squadron.

A member of the ground crew is treading a rather risky path along the fuselage of ED320 as the Lancaster's crew members gather by the main entrance hatch. All but the officer on the right, who is probably the pilot, are wearing the original standard-issue flying boot. The laying of parachute packs on the heavily stained dispersal surface was generally discouraged, since oil or other dirt could fatally erode the canopy in particular. This Lancaster commenced operations in December 1942 but crashed the following August 13.

Operational Expansion

The future of Bomber Command as a viable striking force owed much to a signal event—namely, the first of three 1,000-bomber sorties launched by Air Marshal Arthur "Bomber" Harris on May 30–31, 1942, against the major industrial complex of Köln. The swamping of the defenses by the presence of a bomber stream that included Lancasters, and the resultant heavy damage handed out to this major German city, likely proved the catalyst for governmental approval in terms of progressing with the bombing offensive, however uncertain and costly the campaign might prove to be. A further boost to operations occurred in August with the creation of the Pathfinder Force (PFF), whose function would be to locate and accurately mark targets with flares, a measure that was hoped to lead to more-concentrated and more-destructive bombing. No. 83 Squadron provided the Lancaster element to the four PFF founder squadrons.

The Lancaster element of the Main Force was steadily expanding within the Bomber Command ranks along with the Halifax and Stirling. Their twin-engine predecessors were conversely being phased out of operational service during 1942, although the Wellington—as opposed to the Hampden and Whitley, which would be relegated by April and September, respectively—would soldier on until late 1943. Range, bombload, and generally superior performance enjoyed by the new generation of "Heavies" dictated this necessary transformation.

The initial transformation of the command into a formidable strike force commenced during March 1943 with the first of Harris's planned campaigns, the Battle of the Rühr. The advent of "Oboe," an electronic blind marker system capable of penetrating the permanent smoke layer hanging over this massive industrial zone, ensured that the natural cloak hitherto inhibiting accurate targeting could now be precisely pierced; consequently, the first raid dispatched on March 5–6 to Essen resulted in sizable damage to Krupp's factory complex, among other military production plants. Over the ensuing four months, targets in the Rühr were subjected to varying degrees of punishment. Another electronic device introduced around this time was "H2S"; the device was a plan position indicator that painted a basic black-and-white image of the landscape or water passing beneath the bomber, which was recorded on a set screen. It was initially assigned to PFF aircraft but subsequently became a standard fixture on Main Force bombers and served in the twin role of a navigation and blind-bombing aid. The rotating aerial was housed in a large fairing positioned directly behind the bomb bay.

In late July, Operation "Gomorrah" was initiated, with the industrial capacity of Germany's second-largest city, Hamburg, the focus for a series of raids. The first strike witnessed the introduction of "Window" as a counter-measure to the *Nachtjagd* and flak radar facilities. Thousands of metallic strips cut to a length coinciding with the electronic output of the enemy's equipment were fed into the atmosphere during target approach. The effect was a "blinding" of the radar screens, which inhibited the efforts of the flak guns and searchlights to focus on the formations, while the *Nachtjagd* radar operators' screens were similarly muzzled in any attempt to home in on the bombers. Material destruction was heavy, but the human toll was immense at well over 40,000 fatalities—Total War had expressed itself in its most gruesome manner.

The Lancaster was arguably by now the premier weapon in the Bomber Command's armory. The then-current Halifax variants, although also Merlin powered, were proving to be aerodynamically weak, and it would involve a switch to the radial Hercules before the aircraft began to operate on the same level of efficiency as its Avro cousin. The Stirling's inferior altitude capability was an even-greater operational limitation that would witness its withdrawal from Main Force operations by November 1943.

The final of the three subcampaigns initiated by "Bomber" Harris was directed at Berlin, and although three closely spaced raids occurred in August 1943, the sustained assault is now regarded as spanning November to the following March. During this period the burgeoning threat posed by the *Nachtjagd* fighters, supported by the flak batteries, was to reach its ever-lethal peak during this final battle. Bomber casualty rates had hitherto barely remained below the roughly 5 percent figure, above which the campaign was likely to become unsustainable. The mid-1943 introduction of the *Schräge Musik*, upward-firing cannon mounted on the upper fuselages or in the cockpits of the Ju 88G, Bf 110G, and He 219 night fighters primarily prosecuting the defensive effort, handed the Germans a virtually unchallengeable advantage.

The RAF bombers possessed no ventral defensive equivalent to the USAAF ball turret and were accordingly almost blind underneath. The Lancaster had been originally provisioned with the FN64 turret, bearing two .303-caliber machine guns, but this was deleted early in the bomber's operational career. The presence of the "H2S" equipment in the same location assigned to the ventral turret made the latter's reintroduction impossible on Lancasters so configured; even so, the gunner's field of vision would have been extremely limited, as well as meriting an extra crew member for its permanent manning.

Schräge Musik allowed the fighters to approach from underneath, position themselves usually in line with the wings, and fire into the structure, with a view to setting the aircraft on fire. Such an act

theoretically avoided the target exploding and bringing down both machines had the gunfire been directed into the fuselage, where the bombload could easily erupt if still on hand. Strikes on a partially or fully empty fuel tank probably did induce a similar effect, of course, and could explain the loss of at least one *Experte* (ace). The weapon's presence permitted individual *Nachtjagd* pilots to regularly take down as many as eight bombers during a single sortie.

The RAF aircraft were equipped with passive-warning devices, of which the first was "Monica," located on the rear turret's base. Not only could the signals not differentiate between friendly and hostile machines; worse still was the enemy crews' ability to home in on "Monica" by using a counterdevice code-named "Flensburg." A similar countermeasure code-named "Naxos" was directed at picking up H2S emissions. The combination of these devices and the heavy armament represented by the *Schräge Musik* guns accordingly rendered the cloak of darkness badly if not almost totally redundant as a shield. ("Flensburg" came to light in July 1944, with the fortunate landing on an RAF airfield of a Ju 88G whose pilot had become disoriented; *Schräge Musik*, however, was never similarly uncovered before VE-day.)

One countermeasure intended to subvert the enemy defensive effort initially involved a single unit. No. 101 Squadron was tasked with a specialist role of jamming the German radio control frequency system. Each Lancaster was equipped with "Airborne Cigar" (ABC), whose external existence was confirmed by three long masts, one under the nose and two in a dorsal position behind the cockpit. An extra crew member manned a set that was tuned into the enemy network, and he would attempt to jam any traffic that was picked up. Accounts of the operators confusing the Germans by broadcasting misleading information in German have been discounted; such broadcasts were actually made by personnel based in Britain. "ABC" operations commenced during 1943 and were sustained for the remainder of the offensive.

The "Battle of Berlin" ended with Bomber Command on its back foot, with Lancaster numbers contributing to nearly half of the 1,047 aircraft declared MIA; ninety-five of the overall figure occurred on March 30–31, during a largely failed attack on Nuremburg. It was perhaps as well that the following several months on either side of D-day saw the RAF heavies engaged first in sharing the Transportation Plan with the 8th and 9th US Army Air Forces as well as the RAF's 2nd Tactical Air Force, which rendered largely useless the rail and road links to the Normandy beachhead; this was followed by ground support attacks on the *Wehrmacht* and SS defensive network as the bridgehead was expanded, although assaults on strategic targets such as oil refineries were also indulged in.

On June 20–21, 1943, sixty Lancasters from No. 5 Group launched a long-distance raid on the Zeppelin plant at Friedrichshafen, close to the Swiss border. The raid was notable for what was acknowledged as the first use of a "master bomber." This was a pilot who orbited the target and ensured that the bombs were accurately delivered. The picture shows a No. 49 Squadron aircraft following the raid—not back in Britain but in North Africa, the operation being also the first RAF shuttle run.

One of the features of the design was the ability to remain aloft after sustaining major damage. JA868/PH:U's port wing suffered this strike among other damage inflicted by fighters over Berlin on August 24–25, 1943. Sgt. Knott's crew were fortunate the damage was behind the main spar and clear of the fuel tanks, which lay ahead of the spar. This team completed only seven further operations before they were shot down on their tenth mission over Hannover on September 27–28.

The same seven-man crew shown on the opposite page is now walking away from the Lancaster. The use of Observer-type parachute packs by all seven suggests that this is part of a publicity sequence; pilots tended to wear a seat-type pack attached to the harness, on which they sat during the flight. All but one from among the crew complement sport the original-pattern flying boot.

The seven members of an anonymous Lancaster crew are gathered around the starboard wing of their bomber, on which the ground crew are working within the Merlin engines. The relationship between the two bodies of airmen was one of quiet respect; the ground crew's efforts to maintain their charge in operational order were absolutely key to their airborne colleagues' chances of surviving a tour of duty.

One ground crew member is attending to the FN50 turret while his colleague ensures that he does not slip on what is a smooth and often-slippery surface. The small nature of the aircraft letter was a peculiarity on No. 44 Squadron's Lancasters. The horizontal bar above the letter indicates it is the second applied to a squadron aircraft.

DV397 was a Mk. I Lancaster built in autumn 1943 and dispatched to No. 61 Squadron during November. The stiff breeze indicated by the horizontal windsock will provide a safer run by shortening the distance before the bomber lifts off the runway. An unusual code variation at this stage of the campaign is the repetition of the aircraft letter on the upper fin. QR:W survived operations until the final Berlin strike on March 24–25, 1944.

The airman is beckoning to F/Sgt. Clive Roantree as he brings Mk. III JB632 EA:D into its dispersal at Fiskerton following return from the latest Berlin operation on November 23, 1943. Standard procedure after completing the landing was to taxi on the inboard engines only. The Australian pilot would go on to complete his operational tour, while No. 49 Squadron suffered one of the lowest unit casualty rates during what was a prolonged and extremely costly campaign extending from November 1943 to March 24–25, 1944.

A portrait of "Uncle Joe" Stalin adorns the nose of a Lancaster with twenty Ops symbols as it undergoes engine maintenance. ED382/SR:J was one of 129 airframes built to Mk. I standard and delivered to No. 101 Squadron at Ludford Magna in early 1943. It later transferred to No. 625 Squadron, with whom it saw out World War II. The large wheel-based mobile stands proved a vital factor in carrying out maintenance on the exposed dispersals.

The wheel chocks have been pulled away and the Lancasters of No. 106 Squadron are taxiing out in a fairly close but preordained order as they head for the briefed runway end. This scene of activity was taken at Metheringham during March 1944, with the target being Frankfurt. All but one of the dispatched force landed back several hours later.

Mk. III TL:R, ND759's operational spell with No. 35 (PFF) Squadron was relatively brief. Assigned during March 1944, it was MIA on April 27–28, during an operation to Friedrichshafen. The semisubmerged airframe, lacking its port fin and rudder, rests on the edge of the Bodensee, the large lake on which the target city lies and that separates Germany from northwest Switzerland. Only one fatality was recorded among the seven-man crew, and the bomber's almost-intact state suggests it was ditched.

ND759's relatively intact airframe is clearly demonstrated as it is pulled onto land. The bomber was almost certainly the second claimed this night by *Oblt.* Wilhelm Jöhnen, an *Experte* with *5./NJG 6*. Ironically, the *Nachtjagd* crew in their Bf 110G-4 were subsequently forced to land in Switzerland after the night fighter was set on fire in one engine during a third attack on a bomber. The fire was extinguished and power was switched off; Jöhnen then became disorientated and ended up being forced to land after being coned in Swiss searchlights and facing being shot down by the attendant flak batteries.

The raid on a *Panzer* encampment at Mailly-le-Camp, France, on May 3–4, 1944, cost Bomber Command forty-two aircraft MIA, with several more returning heavily damaged. In this case a No. 576 Squadron Lancaster has come back with the starboard undercarriage collapsing during the landing run. The rear turret's almost complete separation and shot-up state gives little prospect of survival for its recent occupant.

Repair facilities for damaged RAF aircraft were set up at various industrial establishments that in this case belonged to the London, Midland and Scottish Railway Company (LMS) at Derby. Several center-wing frames are being worked on mainly by female staff. Fuselage sections behind belong to No. 44 Squadron (KM) and No. 1651 Heavy Conversion Unit (GP), with an unidentified example in the middle.

ED360 was a Mk. I Lancaster that initially served with No. 467 Squadron until February 1943, when it was transferred to No. 106 Squadron at Syerston, as confirmed by the ZN unit code on the bomb trolley, ready to deliver its load into the gaping bomb bay. An impressive thirty-nine bomb symbols are recorded on the nose, but the bomber's career ended on July 9, when it was burnt out, having by then flown 354 hours on operations.

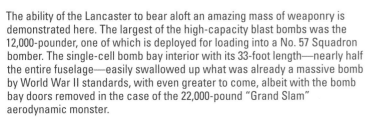

The ability of the Lancaster to bear aloft an amazing mass of weaponry is demonstrated here. The largest of the high-capacity blast bombs was the 12,000-pounder, one of which is deployed for loading into a No. 57 Squadron bomber. The single-cell bomb bay interior with its 33-foot length—nearly half the entire fuselage—easily swallowed up what was already a massive bomb by World War II standards, with even greater to come, albeit with the bomb bay doors removed in the case of the 22,000-pound "Grand Slam" aerodynamic monster.

The crew disembarking at Bardney on return from an extremely protracted run to Stettin on January 5–6, 1944, includes Sgt. Ray Zammitt; the American is the individual wearing the heavily padded yellow flight suit usually worn by air gunners. He will become one of the over 55,000 Bomber Command fatalities barely weeks later. In stark contrast, W4964 (WS:J), nicknamed "Johnny Walker," would complete 106 operations by the following October and be retired to secondary duties.

G-H

The latest in a line of electronic aids arrived during mid-1944 in the form of "G-H," a system that was similar to "Oboe" but functioned in reverse. Unlike "Oboe," which could handle only one aircraft at a time, the new system could be applied wholesale. A further benefit lay in the availability of mobile "G-H" transmitters that moved with the Allied advance and thus extended the range of the equipment beyond the Rühr; the earth's curvature had limited its maximum range to this area prior to D-day. Mobile "Oboe" equipment provided a similar advance.

"G-H" would become a standard feature within No. 3 Group. The aircraft so equipped bore two parallel yellow bars on the fin and rudder, their function being to head a "V" formation, with all three Lancasters releasing their loads on the leader's signal. Operations by the group would steadily intensity from the summer of 1944 onward. Now the cloak of concealment afforded by a heavy or solid cloud base would provide no guarantee of security from assault for the selected target, while the chances of an accurate strike were likely to be greater compared to the use of other more basic electronic devices such as "H2S."

The winter of 1944–45 was one of the worst experienced for years, and the icy conditions facing the crew of a No. 149 Sqdn. Lancaster as they taxi out are rather typical. Ice accretion that could rob the control surfaces of proper function was a constant threat to achieving a secure takeoff run. The aircraft's function as a "G-H" leader is confirmed by the parallel yellow bars on the vertical surfaces.

ED382 was a Mk. I from a mixed batch of Rolls-Royce- and Packard Merlin–powered airframes constructed between November 1942 and March 1943. It is seen bearing twenty symbols for completed operations while stationed at Ludford Magna (No. 1 Group). Unlike over 3,300 of its fellow Lancasters, it went on to survive with the Group's Nos. 625 and 300 (Polish) Squadron, after which it was retired to function with training and instructor units.

NG347/QB:P bears a huge piece of artwork depicting a nubile woman in scanty clothing, but her operational experience along with that of the bomber's was nonexistent. The Lancaster joined the RCAF's No. 424 (Tiger) Sqdn. after VE-day; two indications of its post–European War status are the removal of the engine exhaust shrouds and absence of armament.

The general maintenance of Lancasters, as with all RAF designs in World War II, was largely conducted out in the open, with the personnel being subject to the manifold and often-unpleasant weather conditions. On what is a relatively pleasant day, one airman is precariously perched on a trestle ladder as he cleans the FN5 turret's guns; his companion is cleaning the windscreen. The landing-gear wheel cover bears no tread pattern. The aircraft belongs to No. 44 Squadron, the first to convert onto the Avro bomber and initially based at Waddington but transferring to Dunholme Lodge in May 1943.

The truly prodigious load-carrying capacity of the Lancaster's single-cell bomb bay is amply demonstrated here. A No. 9 Squadron bomber is bearing thirteen 1,000-pound medium-capacity (MC) bombs destined for the Baltic port of Stettin, on January 9, 1944. This weight is marginally more than double the B-17's maximum equivalent and over 50 percent greater than the B-24. Conversely, the unfortunate recourse to nocturnal assault greatly eroded the chances of surgical strikes on industrial or military targets being delivered by Bomber Command, at least until daylight operations were recommenced following D-day.

The twin aerials mounted on a No. 101 Squadron Lancaster's spine, along with a third under the nose, form part of the "ABC" system used as a countermeasure against *Nachtjagd* radio traffic. An eighth crew member would tune into the night-fighter frequencies and attempt to jam them. This extra function was assigned to the Ludford Magna–based unit from late 1943 onward. Also note the Rose-Rice turret with two .50-caliber machine guns.

The airmen busily shoveling snow of a dispersal at Ludford Magna (No. 101 Squadron) are joined by two more engaged in the same duty on the Lancaster's port wing. The need to keep the bomber's surfaces free from snow and ice was vital to ensure that ice accretion did not adversely affect its performance to a potentially lethal degree, especially during takeoff.

The American combat crew members inspecting an incendiary load for a No. 622 Squadron Lancaster based at Mildenhall (No. 3 Group) were visiting from Snetterton Heath, where their B-17-equipped 96th Bomb Group was stationed. The anonymous bomber bears updated paddle-bladed propellers and a larger bomb aimer's Plexiglas frame. The box frame directly behind the Plexiglas is the chute for dispensing the radar-blinding metal strips, code-named "Window."

The aerial supremacy won by the Allied air forces heading toward and following D-day is exemplified by this picture of a No. 300 (Polish) Lancaster tracking over the bomb-smothered target at Bremen on February 28, 1945. A year previous, no RAF heavy-bomber force would have attempted such a strike, since it would have met the full force of the *Jagdwaffe*; now the skies were virtually free of enemy fighter opposition.

The same 96th Bomb Group crew are gathered around the center of the Lancaster's bomb bay as the joint RAF/USAAF party stares up at the 4,000-pound "Cookie" forming the bombload's core. The front of the cylindrical-shaped weapon bears a chalked-on message to whoever might be in the vicinity when it impacts on Third Reich territory. It states in very crude terms ("Duck you B——d") as to how the people so affected should take evasive action, however belated!! These photos were shot in April 1944.

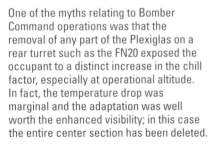

One of the myths relating to Bomber Command operations was that the removal of any part of the Plexiglas on a rear turret such as the FN20 exposed the occupant to a distinct increase in the chill factor, especially at operational altitude. In fact, the temperature drop was marginal and the adaptation was well worth the enhanced visibility; in this case the entire center section has been deleted.

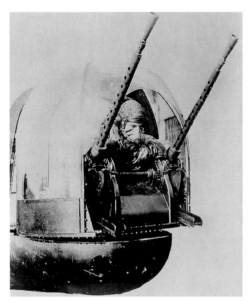

The Rose-Rice rear turret held several key advantages over its FN20 contemporary. First, the twin .50-caliber machine guns provided a better counterbalance to the enemy's firepower. Then, the absence of the mass of equipment facing the FN20 gunner, along with the ability to bring his parachute pack into the roomier Rose-Rice turret, allowed him a far-safer method of abandoning his post in an emergency. Sadly, the new turret was introduced only toward the end of World War II, and then only in small numbers.

The high mortality-rate particularly among air gunners is amply demonstrated here after DV305/BQ:O landed back at Waltham following an Op to Berlin on January 30–31, 1944. The shattered Plexiglas surfaces demonstrates the lethal effect of a Nachtjagd fighter's superior cannon caliber firepower that easily out-ranged the return fire from the .303 machine guns. The mid-upper gunner shared the same sad fate.

External Alterations

The clean outline of the Lancaster was basically retained right through World War II, but several structural and performance changes were introduced during the conflict's latter stages. Falling into the former category were the following: (1) the angled pitot mast's location directly behind the bomb aimer's position was changed to a position at the front of the external strip running the length of the bomb bay and was mounted horizontally, (2) the bubble in the pilot's sliding window panel was deleted, (3) "H" pattern aerials for the "Rebecca" blind-landing system were positioned just ahead of the cockpit windshield, (4) windscreen washer outlets with fairing covers were introduced, (5) the bomb aimer's Plexiglas frame was enlarged to accommodate a more shallowly angled sighting panel for the bombsight, and (6) the main performance advance was the introduction of paddle-bladed propellers in place of the original needle-bladed units, an immediate improvement in climb rate in particular being realized.

The period between briefing and climbing onboard their aircraft was arguably one of the greatest stress stages of any operation. This January 1944 shot depicts a group of air gunners at Ludford Magna, home for No. 101 Squadron. The nervous smile on the individual fourth from left is symptomatic of the tension-laden mindset of the personnel. The yellow kapok suits worn by most if not all present was a standard clothing item for air gunners, who would sadly represent a particularly high percentage of Bomber Command's fatal casualty figure.

A No. 115 Squadron Lancaster has an audience of personnel awaiting its departure on an operation; full power has been applied, to judge by the invisible propeller blades and the brakes released for the takeoff run. No. 3 Group, within which the squadron served, tended to provide different codes for "C" Flight bombers—in this case A4 compared to the "A" and "B" Flight letters KO as seen on the Lancaster in the right background. "C" Flights were utilized to form the cadre of new squadrons within the group during the latter stage of World War II.

The occupants of the houses in this picture, along with all of F/O Crawford's crew on No. 75 Squadron's ND801/JN:X "Get Sum In," were extremely lucky to avoid serious injury or death on February 3, 1945. The Lancaster's wayward momentum after undershooting the runway while completing its eighty-second operation was fortunately spent just before impact with the solid building structures; the pilot and crew members were actually hospitalized following the incident. The row of fuselage windows was permanently deleted on production batches during the course of 1943 onward.

The triangle of searchlights forming a huge cone over Elsham Wolds along with the runway lights provides a dramatic backdrop to ED724 PM:M as the pilot prepares to commence his takeoff run. The No. 103 Squadron Mk. III enjoyed a short operational career between March 1943 and the following month, when it was damaged sufficiently to merit "Category E" treatment.

R5868's original unit assignment was with No. 83 (PFF) Squadron, but by May 1944 it was serving as PO:S with No. 467 (RAAF) Squadron, Waddington. This and the subsequent picture demonstrate the several external alterations applied to numerous Lancasters. Here the bomber bears the early shallow bomb aimer's Plexiglas, with the pitot mast positioned at an angle directly behind and below the frame; the original needle-bladed propellers and the blister in the pilot's sliding window are further features of early-production airframes.

The ninety-eight bomb symbols have expanded to 125 in the second picture as the bomber conducts a 1945 tour of USAAF airfields. A deeper bomb aimer's Plexiglas frame is fitted, while the pitot mast is now located horizontally on the narrow beam directly below the windshield. Replacement paddle-bladed propellers are in place, and the blister in the pilot's fixed window panel is gone. Finally, the H-pattern aerials denote the installation of the blind landing system "Rebecca." Note Hermann Göring's 1940 bombastic statement, which has now been thrown back in his face!

Mk. I R5868 was a prime example of bucking the trend for heavy bombers to survive just an average of eleven operations before going MIA. First with No. 83 Squadron in 1942, it is now seen as PO:S (467 Squadron, Waddington) in mid-1944. Its scoreboard of 100 operations is the reason for the celebratory crowd's presence. The 1940 Hermann Göring statement "No enemy plane will fly over Reich Territory" is a clear refutation of the *Reichsmarschall's* now-fatuous stance.

Mk. I SW244 was adapted to bear additional fuel in a huge Saddle tank extending from the cockpit frame to the wing trailing edges. The likelihood of the Lancasters being dispatched to the Far East and the immense operational distances to be flown were the catalysts for the scheme. Thankfully—for the aircrews' sense of security—no further research was made and it was canceled.

A more complete view of one of the duo of Saddle-tank Lancasters shows the full length of the fitting. This aircraft is seen in the United Kingdom prior to departure for the Far East as a precursor to Operation Tiger, the wholesale detachment of Lancasters to assist in the final assault on the Japanese mainland—an action that was canceled by the Japanese surrender in August 1945.

CHAPTER 3
Lancaster Mk. II

DS604 was the fourth Mk. II airframe produced out of the initial batch of 200, manufactured not by Avro but Armstrong-Whitworth at Baginton. The large Bell-pattern propeller spinner covers were added only from DS628 onward. In addition, the Hercules VI radials borne here were similarly displaced by Hercules XVIs from the same stage of production. The No. 61 Squadron bomber transferred to No. 115, with whom it was lost on April 11, 1943.

The decision to switch an element of Lancaster production to being powered by the Bristol Hercules radial engine was finally confirmed in 1942, following the air testing of the power plant on BT810 the previous November. The contract with Armstrong-Whitworth was for 300 airframes (serial numbers DS601-852 and LL617-739) to be constructed at the company's Baginton factory; production spanned from September 1942 until March 1944, although parallel production of Mk. I/III airframes had already commenced the previous November.

The fourteen-cylinder sleeve-valve engines produced 1,735 hp and were propelled by Rotol airscrews that rotated counterclockwise compared to the opposite direction on the Merlin. The first twenty-seven DS-serial airframes featured the Hercules VI, which was distinguished externally by a shallow, streamlined air intake on top; this contrasted with the XVI, which powered all other Mk. IIs, whose equivalent fitting was the less aerodynamically neat but more efficient operating unit already applied to the Bristol Beaufighter. Bell-pattern spinner covers were also applied to the bulk of the overall production run. (It seems ironic that the Halifax III and VI would conversely switch from the Merlin to the Hercules, the Rolls-Royce engine having enjoyed an indifferent to poor operational career on the Mks. I to V variants of Handley-Page's bomber!)

Apart from the engine switch, a second outline variation on the majority of airframes concerned the bomb bay. The bomb bay doors were bulged from several feet back from the front edge; the conversion was stated to be for the internal accommodation of the 8,000-pound high-capacity bombs then in regular use. The absence of "H2S" sets on all Mk. II airframes permitted the reintroduction of the FN64 ventral turret, although the position

illogically did not merit an extra crew member and so was incapable of being constantly manned—an omission that would surely strike home following the introduction of *Schräge Musik*–equipped *Nachtjagd* fighters! The lighter-weight FN120 rear turret was yet another variation on the Mk. II, although firepower still consisted of four .303s, and the bomb aimer's original, shallow Plexiglas frame remained a standard fitting.

The all-up weight (AUW) at 60,000 pounds on early Mk. IIs matched the Mk. I figure, with the maximum speed at 14,000 feet assessed as 267 mph, and cruising speed as 167 mph. The climb rate was initially better up to 18,000 feet but then fell away to leave the bomber marginally below the level normally sustained by its Merlin-powered brother and therefore more exposed to fighter attack, albeit proving nothing as critical compared to the Stirling. However, the radial engine's air-cooled systems were much less prone to serious (let alone lethal) damage than the oil-cooled Merlin.

Between entry in service in January 1943 and withdrawal during August 1944, a total of five squadrons, comprising three Royal Canadian Air Force (RCAF) and two RAF manned—along with a flight of No. 61 Squadron, which had introduced the Mk. II to operations—operated on the Armstrong-Whitworth bomber. The casualty rate proved almost inevitably high as the squadrons participated in the three battles of 1943–44 as well as the Transportation Plan, the figure amounting to around 60 percent of the 300 bombers involved.

A revised Lancaster variant first appeared in late 1941. The possibility of a production shortfall in Merlin engine production persuaded the RAF to approach Avro with a view to adapting some airframes to operate on the Bristol Hercules radial engine. DT810 was the Mk. II prototype, which not only carried the revised engine design; also fitted is a bulged bomb bay with a single-mounted gun located at the rear end. The light underside color is yellow, denoting a prototype aircraft.

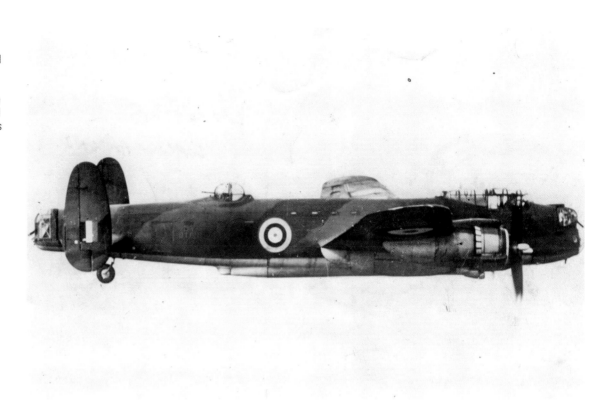

DS869/OW:S, serving with No. 426 (Thunderbird) Squadron, was one of six units equipped with the Mk. II Lancaster. The RCAF Squadron converted from the Wellington in June 1943. The bomber, sporting five bomb symbols, is fitted with the Hercules XVI, which displaced the Hercules VI early in the production sequence. On October 7–8, 1943, it was MIA over Stuttgart. The large Beaufighter-pattern supercharger air intakes were a visual feature of the XVI.

The dark outline of a Mk. II Lancaster prevents identification of the specific squadron in which it is serving. Although the prototype was fitted out with the bulged bomb bay, the initial group of airframes was not so outfitted. The Hercules engine provided a superior platform in climb rate compared to the Merlin, although the exhaust flames were much more of a visual giveaway to the *Nachtjagd* crews.

No. 115 Squadron was one of two RAF units converting completely to the Mk. II Lancaster, No. 514 being the other. The picture angle picks out the parallel walkway lines on the wing surfaces and the row of fuselage windows; the latter were oversprayed on the vast majority of airframes. DS685 was one of thirty aircraft declared MIA on the last Operation "Gomorrah" raid over Hamburg on August 2–3, 1943.

DS723 presents a fine portrait as its pilot lifts his charge off the runway at Linton-on-Ouse, with the undercarriage already beginning to retract. The Mk. II and its crew were stationed here between August 1943 and August 1944, when conversion to Merlin-powered Lancasters occurred. By then, forty-one Mk. IIs had gone down in action, with this machine failing to return from Berlin on November 26–27, 1943.

"Ops are on" is the order of the day at Waterbeach, home for the Mk. II Lancasters of No. 514 Squadron. Eight bombers are depicted as they are prepared on January 3, 1944, for the latest sortie over what was known as "the Big City" by the crews— Berlin! The bulge in the port bomb door on the nearest bomber can be discerned. The closely parked line is unconscious evidence of the *Luftwaffe*'s basic inability to successfully intrude over British soil by this stage of World War II.

Air Vice Marshal (AVM) C. M. "Black" McEwen assumed command of No. 6 (RCAF) Group in February 1944 and held the post until June 1945. He is allegedly snapped directly after return from an operation to Berlin, but this is probably a posed picture, although he did fly in a Mk. II of No. 426 (Thunderbird) Squadron. Officers of this rank and upward were not encouraged to fly for security reasons; many of them were privy to top-level secrets that could be forced out of them should they be captured.

The forward section of a Mk. II fuselage shows the neat outline of the Hercules engines. The large propeller spinner covers were another feature of the Lancaster variant, although a small number of original-production airframes were not so equipped. The barbed engine exhaust pipes also stand out. Another advantage of any radial engine was a greater ability to absorb damage vis-à-vis any in-line contemporary.

The use of inflatable airbags with which to raise an aircraft back onto its undercarriage was regularly indulged in by RAF ground personnel. The Mk. II Lancaster seen here is an early-production machine, the clue being the original more-streamlined supercharger air intakes fitted to the Hercules VIs. Another indication lies with the propellers, which lack the large spinner covers fitted to most Mk. IIs.

The Bristol Hercules power variant used for the Mk. II Lancaster provided an enhanced climb rate, among other features. DS771 was one of the majority from this batch of 200 airframes that was switched from the Hercules VI to the XVI, with its distinctive Beaufighter air scoops. The rear end of the bulged bomb bay can be seen. DS771 lasted on operations until March 15–16, 1944, when it was MIA off a raid on Stuttgart.

The aerodynamic quality of the design is shown here as the pilot maintains flight on a single of the four Hercules engines, albeit with a gentle rate of descent involved. DS794 came from a Mk. II Lancaster batch that featured use of the Hercules XVI with the larger Beaufighter carburettor air intakes on all but the first twenty-seven airframes. The No. 426 (Thunderbird) Squadron bomber lasted from November 1943 until the latest Berlin raid launched on the following February 15.

The USAAF airfield at Leiston on the Suffolk coast was the location for Sgt. Medland's landing attempt on March 17, 1944, while flying a cross-country exercise. The result was severe for the undercarriage, with one of the main wheels seen residing under the starboard wing. The wooden Jablo propeller blades stood little chance of survival in such circumstances. The No. 514 Squadron machine was DS669/JI:K, which is recorded as being restored to operational status only to be MIA on April 22–23.

The rapidly setting sun is casting long shadows in dramatic fashion as a procession of Mk. II Lancasters wait behind the leader on the runway. The propellers form invisible arcs as full power is applied and the brakes are released. Although the artwork is blurred, it seems to accord with that recorded on DS689/OW:S, a No. 426 (Thunderbird) Squadron machine MIA over Stuttgart on October 7–8, 1943.

There is a deceptive beauty reflected in this shot of a Mk. II Lancaster as it wends an aerial path between banks of cumulonimbus clouds. The crew members are undoubtedly settled into their respective positions and functioning accordingly as they head out into the shadowy and dauntingly unpredictable world of airborne battle; the odds against surviving a tour of operations were ever high for the vast bulk of the nocturnal bomber offensive.

The almost surgical removal of this rear turret on a No. 115 Squadron Mk. is mute evidence of friendly-fire risks when operating by night within a bomber stream. The turret has likely been struck by bombs from another aircraft at a higher altitude, the hapless occupant either being killed outright or facing death when his metal enclosure impacted with the ground. Sgt. Jolly (P), kneeling by the gaping hole, was very fortunate that the strike did not land farther forward, with likely adverse effect on elevator function. The picture angle shows the fairing applied to the ends of the bulged bomb bay doors.

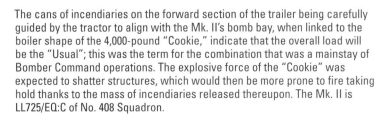

The cans of incendiaries on the forward section of the trailer being carefully guided by the tractor to align with the Mk. II's bomb bay, when linked to the boiler shape of the 4,000-pound "Cookie," indicate that the overall load will be the "Usual"; this was the term for the combination that was a mainstay of Bomber Command operations. The explosive force of the "Cookie" was expected to shatter structures, which would then be more prone to fire taking hold thanks to the mass of incendiaries released thereupon. The Mk. II is LL725/EQ:C of No. 408 Squadron.

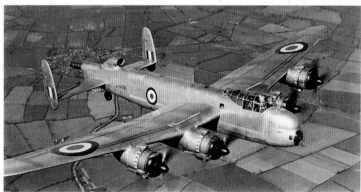

The standard camouflage applied to Lancasters that is absent on Mk. II LL735 is probably due to the airframe being retained for test purposes. In this instance the rear turret is displaced by a Metro-F2/4 Beryl experimental jet engine. Although testing was reportedly commenced during 1943, the type A fuselage and upper wing roundels indicate an immediate postwar period photo.

CHAPTER 4

Lancaster Mk. X

Canada's contribution to Allied success in general and Bomber Command in particular was significant. As regards aerial involvement, No. 6 Group of ACM Harris's command had been assigned to the Dominion's charge in terms both of squadrons and a good proportion of their personnel. A second civilian support effort involved Lancaster production in the form of the Mk. X. In August 1942, the agreement for the Victory Company to turn out the Avro bomber under license was finalized, and L5727 was flown over the Atlantic as the pattern airframe. Apart from further easing the pressure on UK airframe production resources, the scheme also eased the pressure on Merlin production with the availability from US sources of the Packard engine.

It was the following September 1943 before the first of 430 Lancasters (KB700) was rolled out of the factory at Malton, Ontario. It was also the first of seventy-five to be fitted with the Merlin 38; the subsequent 226 airframes from KB775 to KB999 featured the Merlin 224. A similar split affected the choice of propeller types, with the thinner needle-bladed examples superseded by paddle-bladed units from KB775 onward.

KB700, named "Rühr Express," was assigned to No. 405 (PFF) Squadron, having arrived in the UK during October 1943. The "bulged" bomb bay and ventral gun turret seen on the bomber were to prove regular although not exclusive features on the Mk. X; some aircraft were retrofitted with "H2S" following arrival from Canada. Back on the production lines, a number of bombers from later batches were equipped with the Martin turret, bearing twin .50-caliber machine guns, as opposed to the normal FN50 dorsal turret; this in turn created two logistical trails for the aircraft so adapted, which were not compatible with each other should ammunition shortage for either occur during an operation. At least four RCAF squadrons within No. 6 Group operated on the Mk. X, which was exclusively available to this PFF subforce.

The final batch of 130 Mk. Xs was assigned serial numbers from the FM100-229 block, but by April 1945, when production began, the European conflict was virtually over and only FM120 was recorded as reaching an operational squadron, the remainder languishing in various maintenance units (MUs) within the UK. Following the wholesale repatriation of the RCAF squadrons to Canada, these bombers were similarly flown home, but their potential use within "Tiger Force" became redundant when the planned air offensive against Japan was canceled following the August 1945 surrender. Postwar service with Canada's Maritime Command, and as trainers or test beds among several functions, was the lot both for KB- and FM-serial Lancasters.

The decision by the Victory Aircraft Company, based at Malton in Canada, to construct the Mk. X Lancaster was followed by the dispatch of R5727 as a pattern airframe. It is seen immediately prior to departure from Prestwick in Scotland on August 26, 1942. Of particular interest is the FN64 ventral turret, which had a short operational life. R5727's presence on British soil was not at an end, however . . .

. . . R5727's fuselage outline has drastically altered following its return home. The FN5 turret has given way to a framed canopy, the cockpit astrodome has been faired over, and the FN20 rear turret has also given way to a sloped fairing. The pitot mast now resides at the front of the bomb bay longeron, and two D/F loops adorn the lower nose and the cockpit canopy. The top camouflage extends farther down, and the underside Black is replaced by a lighter color. CF-CMS lettering denotes a Canadian civilian status.

The Victory Aircraft Company added to Bomber Command's overall strength by producing 430 Mk. X airframes whose power source was the Packard-built Merlin. These were appreciated by the ground crew because they were usually accompanied by a comprehensive tool kit. This compared positively with the British-built Merlin, where supporting tool kits were rarer than hen's teeth! Mk. X nose turrets were usually faired over, as seen here.

The first Mk. X Lancaster arrived from Canada during October 1943. After evaluation by Avro it was assigned to No. 405 (RCAF) Squadron and is seen taxiing in at Gransden Lodge. The bulged bomb bay can be picked out along with the ventral turret's twin guns drooping down at the back. The bomber survived around fifty operations with this and No. 419 Squadron before being written off in a landing collision—with a steam roller or tractor, according to varied accounts!

The vast bulk of a Mk. X Lancaster squatting outside the production hangars dwarfs the light aircraft snuggling under the nose. KB725 not only has the FN5 turret in place but bears the original-pattern bomb aimer's Plexiglas bubble, which is probably a throwback to the pattern bomber R5727. Note the bulged bomb bay door as evidenced by the crease line toward the rear end.

"X-Terminator" adorns the nose of the No. 419 Squadron Mk. X KB732/VR:X; underneath is the bomb aimer's juvenile nickname. The bomber joined the squadron in June 1944 and when the photo was taken sports seventy-five operations symbols. The oil drum and collection of smaller containers, one of which has a stirrup pump attached, form a typical scene of support clutter to be seen on the average dispersal. An oil wagon can just be seen through the steps of the wooden frame. KB732 was finally struck off charge in 1948.

The strike camera in another bomber caught what is potentially a fatally positioned Lancaster from No. 419 Squadron at seeming risk from being bombed out of the sky by higher-flying companions. The picture angle provides a clear example of the exhaust weathering on the wing surfaces. These ranged from moderate to heavy on all but the outer edges of nos. 1 and 4 engine, where the dihedral deflected most of the exhaust underneath. The red tape masking the dinghy hatch edges also stands out.

The air gunner crouched down on the base of his mid-upper turret is manning the Martin unit fitted to a number of Mk. X Lancasters as well as the postwar Mk. VII (FE). This was sited over the rear of the bomb bay and allowed for an easier exit in an emergency as compared to the normal FN50 turret. The latter was sited back beyond the bomb bay; the access was accordingly more difficult and exit equally so when faced with swift abandonment.

The normal procedure for launching an operation was for the bombers to emerge from their individual dispersals. On this occasion, No. 428 Squadron has a line of aircraft nose to tail on Middleton–St. George's perimeter track. They are fueled up and bomb laden and the crews now await the signal to taxi and take off for Castrop-Rauxel in the Rühr to hammer an oil refinery. The date was November 21, 1944, with the attack made at night.

A party of ground crew members are gathered around the tail turret of KB711, a Mk. X assigned to No. 419 "Moose" Squadron; the squadron shared Middleton–St. George with its Royal Canadian Air Force (RCAF) "twin" No. 428 from November 1942 onward. The outline of the bulged bomb bay on the adjoining Lancaster is clearly depicted. KB711 amassed ninety-two operational hours before being declared MIA on May 1–2, during an operation to St. Ghislain, France.

The bombload carried by this Lancaster demonstrates a variation in the normal explosive/incendiary mix. In place of the canisters bearing the fire-raising weapons are arrayed USAAF 1,000-pound bombs (at front), along with two RAF 500-pound bombs directly behind, and lines of 250-pound bombs enclosing the "Cookie." At the rear are more bombs, making a truly fearsome explosive cocktail for some unfortunate target.

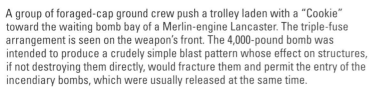

A group of foraged-cap ground crew push a trolley laden with a "Cookie" toward the waiting bomb bay of a Merlin-engine Lancaster. The triple-fuse arrangement is seen on the weapon's front. The 4,000-pound bomb was intended to produce a crudely simple blast pattern whose effect on structures, if not destroying them directly, would fracture them and permit the entry of the incendiary bombs, which were usually released at the same time.

"And Manna fell from the Skies." In late April / early May 1945, the 8th Air Force and RAF Bomber Command delivered critically needed supplies of food and materials to the starving population of still-occupied northern Holland during Operation "Manna/Chowhound." The civilians crowded on streets of an anonymous town gaze upward as two Lancasters head for their allotted drop zones; nearly five years of occupation under an extremely autocratic power are within days of ending, although this is too late for over 25,000 civilians who have died from starvation during the preceding harsh winter.

The RCAF squadrons deployed for Canada within weeks of the war's conclusion. In this aerial view, two Mk. X Lancasters are part of the lineup as they display their well-worn surfaces. Note the late-pattern type C roundels on NA:F, which contrast with NA:G's standard type B markings. The former machine bears a Martin turret equipped with .50-caliber machine guns, while its contemporary sports the FN50, which operated on the smaller-caliber and arguably less effective .303-caliber ammunition.

Having completed a safe crossing of the North Atlantic, KB760/NA:P, "P for Panic," is the center of attention as it taxis in on its inboard engines. What appears to be colored propeller spinner covers was the exception to the rule in Bomber Command—although the Canadians were a law unto themselves, albeit in a reasonably tolerant manner!

A second view of NA:P portside nose section shows the impressive bomb log, totaling at least seventy-two symbols. Of specific interest among the graffiti is the poem applied to the bomb bay door; its theme is that with the European war over, the next task is to eliminate Germany's Axis partner in the Far East—one that will be canceled out by two atomic bombs and Japan's swift surrender during August.

CHAPTER 5
Lancaster Mk. VI

The annular engine cowlings applied to the Merlin 85 and 86 and assigned to the Mk. VI Lancaster are the main distinguishing feature of this variant. DV170, seen here, was one of two from among the small batch of eight that went to Rolls-Royce for engine installation and flight testing. Several aircraft carried out active operations during World War II, the others being retained for various test purposes.

The least-produced Lancaster variant in terms of number (nine) was the Mk. VI. The principal change involved the introduction of the Merlin 85 or 87 engines, with DV170 and 199 being duly fitted out and tested by Rolls-Royce; the annular engine cowlings provided the sole external evidence of the Mk. VI's existence. Seven further airframes were similarly modified to be ready for service trails, of which five entered operational service, and in three cases these served with three squadrons; all these units were part of No. 8 (PFF) Group. No. 635 Squadron was involved with all these Lancasters at some stage, and only JB713 proved the unfortunate exception in being declared MIA on August 18, 1944. Having survived operations, the remaining bombers were allocated to several research sources such as Royal Aircraft Establishment (RAE), Rolls-Royce Hucknall, or the Bomb Ballistics Unit. One of the two bombers not assigned to a squadron (ND479) crashed prior to allocation.

At first sight, this side view of Lancaster JB675 displays the overall outline of a standard Mk. I/III equipped with Merlin 20-series power plants. The one clear feature contradicting this view lies with the barbed exhaust frame on the port outer engine, while the indistinct nature of the picture almost disguises the shape of the annular cowling applied to the 80-series Merlins powering the Mk. VI. The aircraft was assigned to No. 635 (PFF) Squadron, with codes F2:U, and was finally scrapped during 1948.

CHAPTER 6
Lancaster Mks. VII (Interim) and VII (FE)

World War II is over and public displays of RAF aircraft are made available on the September 15 anniversary date of the Battle of Britain. The 1947-period public is patiently lining up to inspect PA385, a Mod. FE version of the Lancaster now serving with No. 214 Squadron. This aircraft originally joined No. 7 Squadron in 1946 but was transferred in December 1946. Its service career was short, since it was scrapped the following April.

The prototype for what was designated the Mk. VII (FE) Lancaster—the letters standing for Far East, with the intention of using these aircraft against Japan—was NN801. The airframe was the forerunner of 230 Lancasters in the NX series to be produced by the Austin Longbridge Company. An intended major external difference was to be the substitution of the hydraulically operated FN50 turret by the US's electrically functioning Martin unit, which would also be positioned farther forward.

In any event, the initial issue of aircraft (NX548/589 and 603/610) ended up as standard Mk. Is, with the British turret in place, due to delays in Martin turret provision; these were granted the title of Mk. VII (Interim). However, the turrets were moved forward to the same location intended for the Martin turret. As matters transpired (with the exception of NX558, which was transferred to Avro), this initial batch was completed in time to participate in active operations over Europe. The repositioning of the FN50 turrets posed problems in fore-and-aft crew movements but, more importantly for the gunner's sake, provided an easier escape access compared to the original location, where the drop to the fuselage base was far greater than the distance to the bomb bay surface.

The main production block (NX611/794) not only involved the introduction of the Martin turret but saw the overall defensive firepower further bolstered. In addition to the twin .50-caliber machine guns in the mid-upper turret was added a similar increase in better firepower as regards the rear turret. The FN20 now gave way to the FN82, which similarly sported twin .50-caliber machine guns. The striking power of both turrets, although halved in weapon numbers in the FN82's case, still provided an enhanced striking power as well as range when confronting an opponent. It is all the more ironic that their qualities would never be tested in earnest.

The notable increase in AUW, set at 72,000 pounds, did not inhibit the Mk. VII (FE) from demonstrating an overall performance akin to that of its Mk. I predecessor. A total of six squadrons took on this Lancaster variant, with the individual unit service in all instances being indulged in abroad during the late 1940s and into the early period of the ensuing decade.

In 1946, No. 35 Squadron was selected to carry out a tour of North America, with the United States a particular focus of attention. W/Comm. Alan Craig, a veteran of No. 8 (PFF) Group, was the CO, and two of the squadron's contingent are seen in pristine condition ready to depart. Note how the "T" of the serial number is repeated underneath in larger scale.

TW657 was the eleventh airframe out of seventy-five produced by Armstrong Whitworth as Lancasters Mk. I (FE) in 1945–46. Assignment to No. 35 Squadron is confirmed in this picture. The standard black-and-white paint scheme is highlighted, as is the FN82 rear turret with its twin .50-caliber machine guns and the serial letters mounted above the number. This aircraft was finally withdrawn from service and dispatched to the firing range at Shoeburyness in 1951.

A pair of Mk. I (FE) Lancasters are seen holding an echelon right formation with the camera aircraft. Both are assigned to No. 35 Squadron and are from a seventy-five-airframe batch built by Armstrong-Whitworth in 1945–46. The postwar black-and-white color scheme is still in good condition, with little exhaust staining emerging yet from the Merlin 24 engines. The row of small fuselage windows is absent here, having been deleted on later-production airframes in the course of World War II. The wing walkway lines extend out to the type C roundels.

RL:L/NX727 commenced production as a Lancaster Mk. VII (FE), as is demonstrated by the Martin mid-upper turret and the bulged bomb bay doors. No. 38 Squadron was serving in the Middle East when this picture was shot, but the operational life of NX727 proved relatively short since it was struck off charge (SOC) in November 1947, for reasons that are somewhat unclear. The code letters and serial are applied in red.

What is probably a Mk. VII (Interim) Lancaster serving with No. 166 Squadron has ended up in an embarrassing position following a heavy emergency landing. The port outer propeller has been wrenched off, as appears also to be the case with the starboard inner Merlin, just visible beyond the nose turret. Color scheme of white and black remained standard on this variant during its RAF service. No. 166 Squadron was disbanded during 1945.

During 1945, Austin Motors produced 200 airframes, with the second subgroup of 150 delivered to Mk. VII (FE) standard. The second airframe from the latter batch so configured was NX612, which never advanced from service with three maintenance units (MU); it served here during 1947 with No. 20 MU 1689 (Ferry Pilot Training) Unit at RAF Aston Down. Of interest is the Martin mid-upper turret, which is positioned farther forward compared to the original location; it lacks the tracking device normally positioned around its base to avoid inadvertent firing into the airframe.

A Lancaster Mk. VII (FE) serving with No. 15 Squadron is seen barely months after World War II's conclusion. The wing commander's pennant beneath the cockpit window belongs to "Jock" Calder (*center*), who will lead the squadron on a goodwill tour of South America; he was the No. 617 Squadron pilot who dropped the first "Grand Slam" on March 14, 1945. An ironic touch is that the engine exhaust shrouds on NX687 have been dispensed with on the Lancasters in the background, now that there is no night-fighter menace from which to shield the bombers.

No. 617 (Dambusters) Squadron switched over from the Mks. I/III Lancaster to the Mk. VII (FE) just after the conclusion of World War II in Europe. However, in contrast to the bulk of its 150 contemporaries within the Austin-produced batch, NX783 did not bear the bulged bomb doors. The squadron moved to India in early 1946 but returned to the United Kingdom in May and quickly converted to the Avro Lincoln.

CHAPTER 7
Pathfinder Force

The creation of an independent Pathfinder Force within Bomber Command was initiated in the late summer of 1942. No. 83 Squadron was part of the four-squadron founding element for No. 8 (PFF) Group, which was based in East Anglia. The picture was taken at Scampton prior to transfer to Wyton and was one of a publicity sequence. The Lancaster in the foreground was declared MIA scant hours after the photograph was shot—just one of 3,346 Lancasters destined to be declared MIA during World War II.

Between the summers of 1940 and 1942, Bomber Command faced the perennial problem of not only locating a target but ensuring that its crews could concentrate their bombloads more effectively. With this in mind, the Pathfinder Force came into being in the early autumn of the latter year, with an initial cadre of four squadrons, each operating on a different bomber design. No. 83 Squadron provided the Lancaster element within this number, but it was soon joined by No. 97 Squadron. Over the ensuing year the Lancaster- and Halifax-equipped squadrons assumed the lead role within what was titled No. 8 (PFF) Group, commanded by Air Vice Marshal (AVM) Don Bennett, an experienced pilot and superbly honed navigation expert.

The initial Pathfinder aircraft would head the bomber stream and release varied patterns of colored flares, which would be sustained by successive waves of PFF crews. The natural vagaries of wind drift and adverse-visibility conditions sometimes resulted in targets being marginally affected by the bomb patterns, while there were instances where the target was barely struck or totally left intact, this being the inevitable result accruing from nocturnal operations. For example, if the cloud base was high, then the flares would tend to be swallowed up and lose their luminosity quickly.

The particular dedication of the men who flew within the group is sharply highlighted by the three Victoria Cross awards granted airmen serving in No. 8 Group out of the overall figure granted to Bomber Command personnel. AVM Bennett had starkly stated that Britain's supreme military award would never be considered for airmen who survived the experience, and this proved to be the case in all three instances.

No. 97 Squadron was another squadron assigned to Pathfinder duties, with Bourn (near Cambridge) the location. The photographer has caught the companion Lancaster with both portside propellers stationary, but the reason for this power reduction is unknown. The heavy exhaust staining on the wing surfaces is evident. No. 97 Squadron was one of the founding units of the PFF.

The bugled fairing under a Lancaster from No. 156 (PFF) Squadron conceals the ground-scanning set code-named "H2S," with which the navigator could determine the approximate—and sometimes almost precise—position of the bomber. The terrain beneath the aircraft showed up dark and light depending on whether land or water was being traversed. The equipment was first used by PFF Stirlings and Halifaxes on January 31, 1943.

No. 635 was formed in March 1944 as a part of No. 8 (PFF) Group, but the duties of E2:Z here are pacific in nature. During May 1945, the Lancasters were part of the force engaged in bringing home POWs, a string of whom are seen at Lübeck, Germany. Note the rear turret in the right background; the bulge houses an Automatic Gun-Laying Turret (AGLT) set that would pick up and engage an encroaching hostile contact. In the center background, a Gloster Meteor jet fighter of No. 616 Squadron can be partially seen behind the Lancaster's undercarriage doors.

The volatile nature of an aircraft, especially one bearing photo flares, among other inflammable resources, is demonstrated by R5549/OF:A. On December 28, 1942, the accidental discharge of these pyrotechnics, probably due to an electrical fault, reduced the Lancaster to a "salvage only" status. The squadron was based within No. 8 (PFF) Group at Bourn when the incident occurred.

A Lancaster pokes its nose out of the T2 utility hangar as King George VI and his wife, Queen Elizabeth, engage in conversation with a line of ground crew, judging by their clothing. The picture is recorded as being taken at Warboys, but no PFF heavy-bomber squadron was officially stationed there during World War II.

PB410 was one of 500 Mk. III airframes powered by the Packard-Merlin engine and produced between May 1944 and March 1945. The aircraft was assigned to No. 97 Squadron, and the picture is taken no earlier than mid-1944; this is confirmed by the yellow-edged code letters, a feature on No. 5 Group Lancasters that was first applied around the inception of the Normandy Invasion on June 6.

ND875, one of 600 Mk. IIIs delivered by Avro in 1943–44, forms the backdrop to a joint aircrew and ground crew photograph at Upwood, home for No. 156 (PFF) Squadron. Note the tail warning antenna above the rear turret and the absence of Plexiglas in the turret's center section; the gunner's enhanced view was well worth the marginal drop in the already frigid temperature level at operational altitude! The bomber was more fortunate than thousands of its contemporaries since it survived the conflict.

CHAPTER 8
The "Dambusters"

The initial testing of Barnes-Wallis's revolutionary weapon was conducted with the assistance of another of the scientist's creations, the Wellington bomber. Two of the test spheres are mounted in the aircraft's bomb bay. The golf ball shape of the bombs did not result in their remaining intact upon impact with the water. Hence the switch to a cylindrical pattern that successfully resisted the surface impact and permitted unimpeded use during the assault on the dams.

No. 617 (Dambuster) Squadron enjoys a distinct place in World War II Bomber Command operations, not least because, unlike any other RAF unit, it was created for a specific purpose—namely, the destruction of a key group of targets, German dams, whose sheer physical scale appeared to render such a feat incapable of completion. The feat was ultimately achieved thanks to the genius of an aviation engineer, Professor Sir Barnes Neville Wallis.

He developed a weapon in the shape of what was not a bomb but rather a sea mine, whose explosive-compressibility factor was expected to rupture the seemingly resistible concrete structures. Early tests in releasing test examples resulted in the initially oval-shaped weapons breaking up on contact with the water surface; a dustbin-shaped replacement proved more structurally effective, but aiming problems still had to be overcome.

The mines had to be released around 600 yards from the dam surface in order to function properly, with their momentum spent at that vital point of impact with the dam wall before sinking to 60 feet and exploding. Moreover the release-height factor was just 60 feet. The aiming difficulty was solved with the aid of a Y-shaped frame with holes at the top, through which the bomb aimer focused; once the holes in the tops of the "Y" were aligned with the twin towers on the dam, he released the mine. An alternative was the placing of vertical chinagraph lines on the bomb aimer's Plexiglas frame, similarly intended to line up with the towers at the release range. The height limitation was solved by two fuselage-mounted lights focusing down on the water surface to join up at the required height.

Led by W/Comm. Guy Gibson, a veteran pilot with Nos. 83 and 106 Squadrons, nineteen Lancasters took off on May 16, 1943. The Lancaster bomb bays had been modified to accommodate a V-shaped frame holding each mine with a mechanism that would spin the weapon backward on release, an action causing it to skim across the water surface in the manner of a flat stone being similarly projected.

Nine crews headed toward the Möhne and Eder dams east of the Rühr industrial complex, while five were directed against the Sorpe, with the remainder allocated to other structures. A brilliant result was realized at the first two locations, although two crews were lost during the respective assaults and two more were lost on either side of the assault's delivery. Only two of the Sorpe attackers reached the site, with minimal damage inflicted on the compacted earth structure, which was immeasurably more resistant to seismic effect compared to the concrete-based Möhne and Eder dams, while four more crews from this and the other projected assaults went missing in action.

Added to the severe casualty rate was the relatively short-term effect on German economic resources. More tangible from an Allied viewpoint was the upsurging effect on the British public's morale, and the likely downturn in morale on their German contemporaries, whose leaders could not guarantee security from future equally threatening aerial disruption delivered in similarly precise form. Guy Gibson received the Victoria Cross, and the squadron's future as a pinpoint specialist unit was basically assured.

ED817 was one of a number of Lancasters suitably modified for No. 617 Squadron's planned assault on the Möhne, Eder, Sorpe, and three other barrage dams in or east of the Rühr industrial complex. One adjustment was removal of the mid-upper turret, whose location is faired over and whose occupant would be up front in the FN5 nose turret; his brief was to suppress any flak fire encountered on or around the dams. This bomber did not participate in the raid, however.

The depth-charge weapon was mounted between V-pattern yokes. A drive mechanism with a cog fitted ahead of the yoke was equipped with a belt whose rear end fitted onto the weapon's central spindle. The belt's operation spun the weapon backward, an action that permitted it upon release to skip across the water. Dropped at a distance where its momentum would be spent coincidentally with the dam wall, it would sink to a depth of around 60 feet, where the hydrostatic pistol would activate the explosive content.

The fitting of the drive mechanism to the nineteen Lancasters assigned to Operation Upkeep merited the detaching of the bomb bay doors and a sloped fairing at the rear of the bay. Although none too clear, the belt drive can be seen directly below the starboard inner Merlin. This specific bomber did not participate in the raid.

The original release height of 150 feet was low enough, let alone being subsequently reduced to a mere 60 feet. The picture shows the practice run of a Lancaster at the revised operational height. One risk not really foreseen was the splash effect of the water, which in one case impacted with the bomber's rear fuselage, damaging the elevators and making the resultant flight and landing approach a very dangerous activity, as the pilot, F/Lt. Les Munro, later explained!

The officer assigned to command No. 617 Squadron was the veteran pilot Guy Gibson. He is seen with hands in pocket when commanding No. 106 Squadron the morning after the raid on Köln by 1,047 bombers. Gibson would fly more than 160 sorties during World War II before heading to Scampton to take up his new appointment. This squadron was converting from the Manchester, two of which are parked in the background.

W/Comm. Gibson pauses as he enters AJ:G prior to the raid. Although the crew returned to Scampton, none would survive the conflict. Of the six other airmen, four would die the following September on the way to bomb the Dortmund/Ems Canal. F/Lt. Trevor-Roper (L) would be MIA on March 30–31, 1944, during the disastrous Nuremberg raid. Gibson was the final casualty when serving as master bomber on September 19–20; his Mosquito impacted at Bergen-op-Zoom in southwestern Holland, killing him and S/Ldr. Warwick (N).

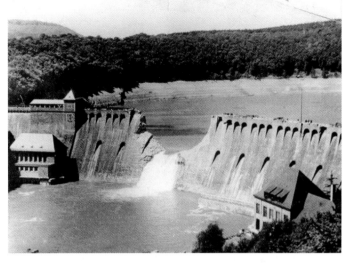

A postoperation view of the Möhne dam starkly reveals the scale of the breach in the structure, the depth of which extends well over half of the dam's vertical height. The several barrage balloons now raised only confirm the belated nature of this defensive measure, which could have lethally hindered the Lancaster crews' approach had they been present at the time. Truly a case of "shutting the stable door after the (aerial) horse had bolted"!

The run-in to the Eder dam was immeasurably more difficult than with the Möhne. The open, extended approach to the latter-named target contrasted starkly with the foreshortened time factor over the Eder; this was due to the bombers having to make a steep descent and level off with scant time in which to set up the bomb run before reaching the release point. The problem is highlighted by the offset nature of the breach compared to the central strike on the Möhne structure.

In 1954, production was commenced on the film *The Dambusters*, which recalled Operation Chastise—the attack on the major dams east of the Rühr on May 16–17, 1943. The available Mk. VII Lancasters were appropriately modified, but the actual weapon was not displayed since it was still on the Secret List. The extension of the code letters onto the top camouflage is incorrect, while the Mk. VII's FN82 turret did not come into service until well after the operation took place.

The film company concerned with producing *The Dambusters* was fortunate that the Lancaster was still in RAF service at the time. However, these were Mk. VII variants bearing the later-pattern FN82 rear turret and extended astrodome at the rear of the cockpit. The essential overall shape of the Avro bomber was retained, however. This example flying low over the crowd is NX671, which in two years would be gone into retirement along with all its contemporaries.

The "Dambusters" raid is regularly commemorated as a leading example of Bomber Command's prowess in striking home effectively against its World War II adversary. In this instance the Battle of Britain Memorial Flight (BBMF) Lancaster is seen traversing a dam in northern England that sports a similar twin-tower layout to the Möhne. The photographer has caught the shadow of the bomber on the dam's sloping surface as it symbolically overshoots the structure.

"Tallboy" and "Grand Slam"

The RAF were far ahead both of the US and their *Luftwaffe* adversary in developing bombs that were not only massive in destructive capability but were moreover superb aerodynamic designs. The credit for their existence once again emanates from the fertile brain of Barnes Wallace. The first of these was a 12,000-pound missile whose dimension of around 18 feet ensured that only the Lancaster could accommodate it within its bomb bay. This was named "Tallboy," and its function was radically different from any previous bomb. In contrast to a standard bomb, which expended its explosive energy on the surface, this weapon would delve up to 100 feet or more into the soil before impacting. The result would be a "hangman's drop" effect that would destroy the foundations of the selected target.

An initial use just after D-day against a railroad tunnel southwest of Paris proved the point, as did subsequent attacks on targets such as the E-boat pens at Le Havre and projected V-3 facilities in northeastern France, which were rendered totally out of action. The single most notable success involved the battleship *Tirpitz*, which fell victim to the "Tallboy" on November 12, 1944. However, it was the even more colossal successor to "Tallboy" that underscored the effect of Barnes Wallace's weaponry.

"Grand Slam" weighed in at a colossal (by World War II standards) figure of 22,000 pounds, of which 55 percent was explosive content; it was capable of being hoisted aloft only by the Lancaster. Even then, the bomber had to shed its bomb bay doors and have an adapted bomb bay structure installed to accommodate the bomb securely. The bomber shed all but the rear turret, with other extraneous equipment removed before the first operation could be launched.

On March 14, 1945, F/Lt. "Jock" Calder lifted off, with his bomber's wing dihedral flexed upward in a dangerously extended manner. He headed out for the railroad bridge at Bielefeld, northeast of the Rühr, but the altitude reached on target approach was still well below the recommended minimum height for successful effect. Nevertheless, the bomb was released; the immediate result was apparently visually disappointing, but subsequent examination revealed that several pillars of the bridge has been totally destroyed, thus ensuring that its repair would be massive and long term. The operation was the first during which forty further "Grand Slams" were delivered with equal effect prior to VE-day.

The second-heaviest bomb used by the RAF, and capable of being stowed only internally by the Lancaster, was the Barnes-Wallis aerodynamic creation titled "Tallboy," which weighed in at 12,000 pounds. The precision weapon was used against pinpoint targets and was allotted to Nos. 9 and 617 Squadrons. Its first use was against a railway tunnel southwest of Paris in June 1944, but arguably the key successful strike involved the sinking of the battleship *Tirpitz* on November 12, 1944, while it was berthed at Tromsø fjord in northern Norway.

Barnes-Wallace's second aerodynamic creation was a veritable monster that weighed in at 22,400 pounds, almost double that of the "Tallboy." Named "Grand Slam," the overall length was 25 feet, 5 inches, and the explosive content was 9,200 pounds of Torpex. One among a group of five is being carefully maneuvered by a Coles Crane and will be loaded on a specialist trolley for transport to the selected bomber.

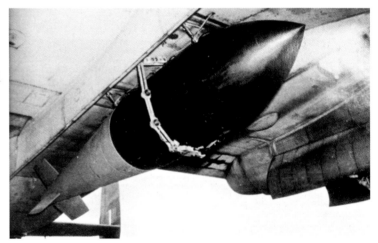

W/Comm. Willy Tait (*fourth from right*) stands with a crew from No. 617 Squadron, of which he was then the CO. The eight airmen have just participated in the destruction of the *Kriegsmarine*'s last capital ship threat in the form of the *Tirpitz*, which was sunk by this and No. 9 Squadron on November 12, 1944. The Lancaster in the background has the mid-upper turret deleted to reduce the overall AUW, while it bears the "C" Flight codes of KC.

The girth of the "Grand Slam" was too great for it to be enclosed even within the Lancaster's massive bomb bay. The doors were detached and both ends of the bomb bay were revised with sloping surfaces. Note the extra retention factor in the form of a heavy chain to supplement the normal fittings in the bomb bay roof. The bomb penetrated and exploded up to 200 feet underground, the shock effect acting like a "hangman's drop" to excise the foundations of the target in question.

The B Mk. I (Special) on No. 617 Squadron bore a different camouflage scheme, as seen on this example that is ready to receive its "Grand Slam." The Black color scheme on the undersides gave way to a Grey tone, while the top Dark Earth and Green pattern was extended down to near the base of the fuselage. The Specials also carried a separate "YZ" code letter combination. Armament was restricted to two guns in the rear turret, with the mid-upper turret deleted and the nose unit faired over.

The picture quality is somewhat grainy but still captures the stark drama of a "Grand Slam's" release from the B Mk. 1 (Special) sculpted bomb bay. The original minimum altitude for an effective strike was short by several thousands of feet in practice but was still adequate for the full destructive effect of the dropped bombs to be felt. This photo was extracted from a film sequence, and what is missing here is the manner in which the loss of 10 tons of weight caused the Lancaster to soar completely out of the camera lens's visual orbit! Note that the bomber carries standard camouflage compared to the normal B1 (Special) temperate scheme.

PD119/YZ:J demonstrates the comparatively clean top fuselage outline with the deletion of the FN50 mid-upper turret. Note how the rear turret retains its full complement of guns while the port fin and rudder are still left Black. Exhaust shrouds have been removed, among other measures to lighten the overall airframes on the B Mk. I (Special). The application of squadron code letters to the horizontal stabilizer was a feature on several No. 5 Group squadrons.

The myriad of standard bomb craters surrounding the twin-structured railway viaduct at Bielefeld, northeast of the Rühr, is supplemented by several massive "Grand Slam"-inflicted strikes. The latter have pulverized several pillars to render the viaduct totally useless. On March 14, 1945, the target was the first to suffer the effect of the massive bombs. Although VE-day was then less than two months distant, a specific measure of disruption to the German transport network was still administered.

A total of forty-one "Grand Slams" were released in anger prior to cessation of Bomber Command operations. In this scene a B Mk. I (Special) is involved in striking at another major rail target. The photograph purports to show the viaduct at Arberger, near Bremen, which suffered two strikes on March 21. The destructive effect was positive despite the Lancasters being unable to gain anywhere near the theoretical minimum height deemed necessary for the weapon to succeed in the planned manner.

A section of Lancasters from No. 617 Squadron demonstrate the variation between a Mk. I/III and a B Mk. I (Special). The duo falling into the latter category reveal the sculpted bomb bay minus its doors, which was necessary to accommodate the 22,000-pound "Grand Slam." Note also the different code letters and extended top camouflage on YZ:B and YZ:J. KC:B's sole alteration from the standard Lancaster's outline is the bulged bomb bay doors, which permitted the enclosed carriage of the 12,000-pound "Tallboy."

CHAPTER 9
Postwar Lancasters

The end of the European war on May 8, 1945, did not immediately result in the grounding of the Lancaster in particular; instead the bombers were used to bring home POWs as well as British army personnel serving in Italy. Preparations were on course for "Tiger Force" to transfer to the Pacific, with a view to its Lancaster squadrons participating in the projected assault on Japan, but that nation's surrender in August spelled the cancellation of operations.

A new role for the Avro design involved not land but maritime operations, which would see the aircraft's continued service up to 1956. The Air-Sea Rescue (ASR) was the first of three variants that would serve in this specific role. The Lindholme lifeboat was a key aspect of operations, being borne under the ASR Mk. III's fuselage and released to float down under parachute assist. The General Reconnaissance (GR) and Maritime Reconnaissance (MR) contemporaries enjoyed a more general function in patrolling the sea lanes in search of submarine activity, in particular during the 1940 and early 1950s, with the West's former ally, Soviet Russia, ironically now the principal adversary.

Despite the wholesale scrapping of airframes, the relative plethora of late-production Lancasters still on hand caught the eye of Britain's expanding civilian aviation world. The aircraft's availability both for civil airline and attendant engine development was eagerly seized on. In the former case, a number of airframes were adapted for passenger use, with the title Lancastrian applied. Turrets were removed and nose and tail cones were applied, along with enlarged window frames. In the case of engine development, a mix of jet- and turbine-powered examples were mounted either in place of the Merlins or in the bomb bay or were borne on adapted nose frames.

The arrival of the Lincoln, a larger Avro version powered by the Rolls-Royce Griffon, during the late 1940s did not mean the end of the Lancaster's presence within RAF operational circles; it was the introduction of the jet-powered Canberra in the early 1950s that was the true catalyst for the withdrawal of both Avro designs from frontline service. However, Coastal Command's use of the Lancaster was more measured in terms of final exclusion. It was October 1956 before the Lancaster was finally withdrawn from frontline RAF service, when RF325, a GRIII conversion serving with the Anti-submarine Warfare Development Unit (ASWDU), departed from St. Mawgan for ultimate scrapping.

The surrender of Nazi Germany has been confirmed and the men of Bomber Command can anticipate a return to a normal life span—unlike over 55,000 of their contemporaries who had been sacrificed in order to achieve the peace. The nose area of a Lancaster and the searchlights forming a "V for Victory" sign sum up the nation's effort.

"Exodus" was the code name for the large-scale repatriation of Royal and Commonwealth Air Forces' POWs. No. 463 (Australian) Squadron's JO:V has had its letters absorbed into the words "By Jove"—a British expression denoting support for a positive outcome, with the recent conclusion of hostilities a clear example! Chalked messages are liberally applied to the fuselage. Yellow-edged letters and repetition of the aircraft letter on the fin were features on No. 5 Group Lancasters from mid-1944 onward; chalk lines within the letters and the roundel face are unofficial additions.

No. 103 Squadron's ED888/PM:M2 rises gracefully aloft, having already cleared the runway prior to reaching the intersection, its light-laden condition having allowed this to happen. Known as "M-squared" or "Mother of them all," it held the Bomber Command's record for operations (140), beating R5868/PO:S by three. Sadly, unlike R5868, it was not preserved and was unceremoniously scrapped along with numerous of its contemporaries two years after World War II.

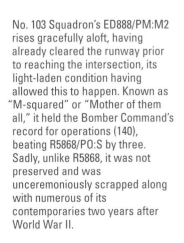

The tail has been raised to get the rudders into play as a Lancaster PA238/SR:J from No. 101 Squadron gathers speed to lift off the runway. The occasion is the RAF's concerted effort to bring its POW complement back from their former locations of internment, and home to British soil. The aerials for the specialist ABC system have already been withdrawn on this particular Lancaster. The red-fringed yellow disc on the nose was a gas-warning symbol peculiar to bombers serving with No. 1 Group in Bomber Command during World War II.

The end of World War II did not witness Barnes-Wallace's "Grand Slam" bombs becoming immediately redundant. No. 15 Squadron was assigned Lancaster B1 (Special), one of which is seen being inspected by USAAF personnel at RAF Mildenhall; the shape of the huge weapon can just be discerned. The fortified island of Helgoland off the northwestern coast of Germany possessed U-boat pens, and these became the focus for test drops of the bombs during 1945–46. Several of these weapons are still reportedly held at the US Air Force Museum in Dayton, Ohio.

No. 203 Squadron was created during 1947, and a GRIII category was allocated to SW377; in addition, it was configured to an ASR standard by the attachment of a Lindholme motorized lifeboat, as demonstrated in the photograph. Only the FN5 nose and FN82 tail turrets are retained but no armament is installed. What looks like a second pitot mast is applied under the forward nose compartment.

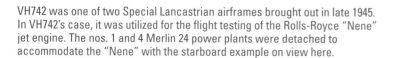

VH742 was one of two Special Lancastrian airframes brought out in late 1945. In VH742's case, it was utilized for the flight testing of the Rolls-Royce "Nene" jet engine. The nos. 1 and 4 Merlin 24 power plants were detached to accommodate the "Nene" with the starboard example on view here.

The Lancaster's original row of small windows, which were fitted with a view to the aircraft possibly being used as a military transport, were deleted on production Lancasters during 1943. In the case of the Lancastrian, the reintroduction involved apertures that were located lower down but expanded in size in order to meet with civil aviation requirements. The aircraft seen here belongs to an Italian concern, as confirmed by the lettering as well as the national colors displayed as a fin flash.

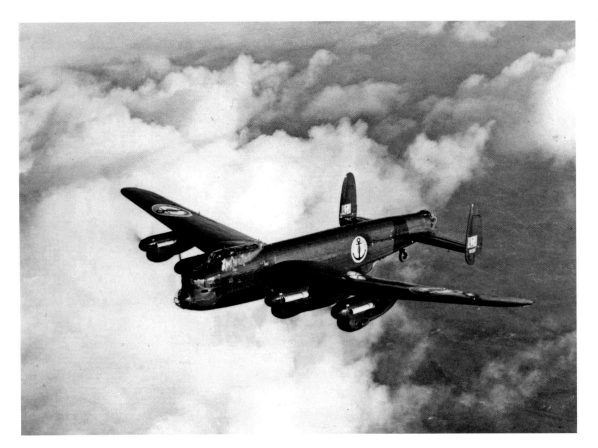

The *Aeronaval* (French navy) requisitioned and took on fifty-four Lancasters from several production blocks between 1951 and 1954. The batch, with their distinctive anchor inserts within the national markings, bore either the Dark Blue overall color scheme or alternatively were sprayed overall White. This WU-33-coded aircraft was originally PA477; note the clear Plexiglas cover to the radar equipment.

The art of midair refueling gathered pace after World War II, especially when given the very thirsty nature of the jet engine's fuel consumption. In this instance a Lancaster has been converted to the function and is carrying out the test duty for a Mk. IV Meteor. Points of note are the foreshortened nose and faired-in tail sections, and the astrodome above the rear fuselage.

Canada

By far the largest postwar overseas operator of the Lancaster was Canada, but this was hardly surprising given the Mk. X production output from the Nation's Victory Aircraft plant during World War II. The sizable Pacific and North Atlantic coastlines merited regular maritime reconnaissance, with the Lancaster as a suitable choice. One of the eleven variations now designated Mk. 10-, the 10-MR (Maritime Reconnaissance) was the original designation for the airframes allocated to the duty, but a title change to MP (Maritime Patrol) was subsequently introduced. Lancasters allocated to a 10-AR (Arctic Reconnaissance) role featured a lengthened nose and were fitted with radar and camera equipment.

Thirteen aircraft were categorized under the 10-BR (Bomber Reconnaissance) title, while nine were modified for photoreconnaissance and mapping operations (10-P) and eight were tapped for Air-Sea Rescue (10-SR). Specialist duties included two 10-DCs (Drone Carriers), three 10-Ns (Navigation Classrooms), and a single 10-O used for flight testing the Avro/Canada "Orenda" turbojet. A civilian use of the Mk. X involved an unspecified number of airframes converted for operation by Trans Canada airlines. Finally, the 10-U term was applied to a reserve pool for potential allocation to one of the foregoing groups, while 10-S was the term for either museum-allocated Lancasters or airframes held in reserve and intended to be utilized for spare parts.

FM219 was one of a batch of 130 out of a projected figure of 200 Mk. X Lancasters produced by the Victory Aircraft of Canada concern between April and August 1945. It was modified to serve in a Maritime Reconnaissance role with No. 407 (RCAF) Squadron. This specific aircraft was still on hand in 1959, although it was then recorded as being held at a depot of some sort. The tail turret has been faired over, with the nose turret left clear for observation use. The large-sized black code letters are prominently displayed.

The annular engine cowlings of what is a Mk. VI Lancaster confirm its use as an engine test bed. In this case the former bomber's nose compartment is deleted in order to accommodate an Armstrong-Siddeley "Mamba" power source. The engine proved very efficient and was doubled up in format for assignment to the Fairey Gannet antisubmarine aircraft.

The Canadian Mk. X Lancasters served in nine active postwar roles, one of which was as a photographic reconnaissance and mapping aircraft. KB868 had originally served with No. 431 Squadron from March 1945 until VE-day; the retention of what looks like the H2S pod behind the bomb bay reinforces it status as a World War II–vintage production airframe. The official designation for this aircraft's function was 10P.

Lancaster PA474 was produced too late to become operational in World War II but was destined to become almost unique—it was and still is one of only two fully airworthy examples of the Avro bomber in existence. It was converted to PR Mk. I standard and served with No. 82 Squadron. Another role was serving as a test bed for laminar-flow wing design, as seen here. This function was carried out at Cranfield's College of Aeronautics.

The location is the Coastal Command airfield St. Eval in southwestern England on October 15, 1956; the Lancaster is ASR Mk. III RF325. The significance of the ceremony now unfolding relates to the Avro aircraft's final removal from RAF service. Nearly fifteen years of crucial availability in war and peace have been realized. Now the aircraft will depart for a depot and reduction to scrap metal, but the design will deservedly live on as a historic and national icon.

Lancaster Mk. I R5868 stands in splendid prominence within the Bomber Command section of the RAF Museum in north London. Its log of operations totals an incredible 137 in number; this is all the more amazing when one considers it first entered active service in late 1942, to soldier on through the 1943–44 period. Increasingly severe casualty rates in bombers and crews were incurred during this extended period. The aircraft is truly a fine tribute to all who flew and serviced it and its contemporaries during World War II. Note the 12,000-pound bomb underneath; this was the forerunner of the more aerodynamically shaped precision weapon, the "Tallboy."

The Battle of Britain Memorial Flight's (BBMF) Lancaster joined the unit's strength in the late 1960s, and has been a central feature ever since. The bomber is banking gracefully toward the camera and displays the standard World War II camouflage pattern in the process. One item currently missing is the red tape surround to the dinghy hatch located on the starboard rear wing and just outboard to the fuselage/wing joint. The starboard-side pair of .303-caliber machine guns in the rear turret is for some reason absent.

The BBMF Lancaster's unit identity is changed every year or so; the intention is to cover as many Bomber Command squadrons' insignia as possible. In this instance the aircraft bears the code letters for No. 9 Squadron, while the artwork relates to the original "J for Johnny"; this was W4964, which survived a phenomenal total of 106 operations at Bardney between January 1943 and late 1944 before being retired to ground instruction duties. Yellow-edged codes were a feature on No. 5 Group bombers from mid-1944 onward; a white fin was a squadron marking added around the same period of operations.

As with the BBMF's Lancaster, so this Mk. X KB889 was destined to live on as a Bomber Command exhibit, albeit in static form at the Imperial War Museum, Duxford. Its postwar role was with Canada's Maritime Air Command, as confirmed by the logo on the lower nose. The FN5 turret and rear cockpit frame are faired over, while what appears to be a radar scanner with a parallel-sided cover is mounted behind the bomb bay. The white and NMF-finish fuselage with a thin arrowheaded separation strip and red outer-wing sections were standard features on these RCAF aircraft.

The very distinctive and colorful scheme applied to the Mk. X in postwar service with the RCAF is fully captured in this picture of KB976. Assigned to No. 405 Squadron but too late to see any action, the aircraft was allocated the role as a 10-AR (Arctic reconnaissance) with No. 408 Squadron. The basic NMF finish is shared with a white upper fuselage with a thin double-red separation line, red stabilizers, outer wingtips, and spinner covers. Some 10-ARs featured extended nose sections with a fairing replacing the nose turret, as seen here; the lower nose bears the legend Air Transport Command even though records indicate its allocation to 10-AR duty. The aircraft was finally scrapped in 1955.

KB726 bears the Martin mid-upper turret with twin .50-caliber machine guns, which displaced the standard RAF's FN50 .303-caliber turret equivalent. It was from this location that F/Sgt. Mynarski (posthumously promoted to P/O) began to abandon the doomed Lancaster but then vainly attempted to rescue his fellow gunner and close friend P/O Brophy, trapped in the jammed FN20 rear turret, an act that later culminated in his succumbing to burns incurred during his self-sacrificial deed. Amazingly, Brophy survived when the turret became separated following the bomber's violent impact with the ground.

This superb photograph depicting KB726/VR: A—with whom the B-17G "Thunderbird," based in Galveston, Texas, and bearing the original 303rd Bomb Group markings, is maintaining a tight echelon formation—unconsciously epitomizes the spirit of the Combined Bombing Offensive conducted over Europe in World War II. Both Allied Bomber Commands played a vital part in hammering Nazi Germany's industrial potential to the point where its overall efficiency was fatally weakened, albeit at a high cost in material and human resources.

As with the BBMF's PA474, the Mynarski Lancaster X is also maintained in airworthy condition as a living tribute to the thousands of airmen assigned to RAF and Commonwealth squadrons within Bomber Command. A major difference with the Canadian bomber is its ability to accommodate passengers; whereas PA474's interior has all the World War II equipment in place, KB726 is only partially restored in this manner, thereby having more than enough spare space in which to install seating.

This picture fully encompasses the relationship between the Avro Company's involvement in heavy-bomber production both during World War II and in the postwar era. The BBMF's Lancaster has just overflown the hangar housing the last airworthy Vulcan jet bomber, one of three "V"-named jet-powered designs that formed Bomber Command's nuclear strike force from the 1950s onward. The cameraman has precisely caught the image of the delta-winged bomber from the World War II veteran machine's rear turret.

The Canadian government's involvement in Lancaster production as well as the equipping of an entire Bomber Command Group (No. 6) during World War II is commemorated by the sole other airworthy machine in current existence. KB726 is maintained in perfect condition, its Mk. X status visually confirmed by the Martin mid-upper turret. The markings relate to the No. 419 Squadron bomber on which F/Sgt. Andrew Mynarski won a posthumous Victoria Cross in mid-June 1944.

The picture of two Lancasters taxiing along a perimeter track is one that may well never be repeated. The scene is not World War II vintage but an airfield location in Britain during the summer of 2014, when the Canadian War Heritage brought their Mk. X KB726 over to Britain. It is following closely behind the BBMF's PA474 as the duo prepares for the latest in their comprehensive range of displays across the length and breadth of the nation.

The Marstrand antishimmy tailwheel is one tragically mute indicator that the several bystanders collected around the wreckage are gazing upon the rear section of a downed Lancaster. The crash site is quoted as being Grange-sur-Vologne, a town roughly 35 miles southeast of Nancy in southern France. The exact details of the bomber's loss and fate of its crew are not known to the author, but it is sadly unlikely that all or indeed many of the airmen escaped with their lives, given the huge scale of fatalities among the World War II ranks of Bomber Command.

Ten of the sixteen Victoria Cross awards to Bomber Command aircrew went to Lancaster crew members. On January 1, 1945, F/Sgt. George Thompson's No. 9 Squadron Lancaster was set on fire. The radio operator fought his way back through the flame-drenched fuselage to rescue Sgts. Haydn-Price and Potts from their turrets; Potts subsequently died, and although Thompson survived the crash landing, the burns he sustained during his gallant efforts claimed his life several weeks later when he died in the hospital from pneumonia. His award stands as a standard for the self-sacrificial acts of him and his medal-winning fellow airmen, half of whom did not emerge alive during the conflict.

The scene of a Lancaster crew depicted here could have been taken during World War II. In fact this shot is recorded long after the events of the RAF's Bombing Campaign, although it is taken at East Kirkby, a former No. 5 Group airfield. "Just Jane" is a B Mk. VII/NX611 currently owned by the Panton brothers, who own the site. The aircraft serves as a memorial to their elder brother who died on operations in a Halifax on March 30–31, 1944. The aircraft is not currently airworthy, although it can be taxied and accelerated to a point where the tail lifts off the ground. Tentative plans are in hand to bring it up to airworthy condition.

Luck of the draw. The ever-slim margins between survival and death while operating within RAF Bomber Command are sadly exemplified by the two aircrew members serving as air gunners on No. 9 Sqdn., based at Bardney within No. 5 Group. They will be participating in one of the Operation "Gomorrah" raids on Hamburg. Sgt. Jack Dickinson (RCAF) will return to Canada on completion of his operational tour; his NCO companion, Sgt. Gilkes from Trinidad (**right**), will add to the horrendous scale of fatal casualties borne by the flight personnel in securing final victory for the Allies.

Aeronaval (French Navy)

A major user of the Lancaster from among four non-Commonwealth sources was France, with the focus being on airframes equipped for maritime patrol duties. A total of fifty-four aircraft were suitably modified and numbered WU1 to WU54, with delivery commencing during 1951. The original *Aeronaval* dark-blue overall scheme was later switched to overall white, the aircraft so modified being intended for operations in more-tropical regions. Final delivery was completed during 1954. The service provided by the Avro bomber extended as far as 1964, with one unit based in New Caledonia; otherwise, steady replacement by and conversion to, in particular, the Lockheed P2V Neptune, a custom-designed maritime aircraft, spanned the period of the late 1950s into the early 1960s. At least nine naval squadrons operated the Lancaster during its existence, with the French navy flying from bases between France, North Africa, and the Far East.

Argentina, Egypt, and Sweden

A further total of twenty-five Lancasters were shared out between three countries, with the largest proportion (fifteen) making the extremely protracted flight from Britain to Argentina between mid- and late 1948. Three were modified to a transport function. Of the remaining ten, all but one were dispatched to serve with the Egyptian military, following an order placed during 1948 and completed in 1950. Sparse records exist of how they were utilized, although it was reported that two-thirds were reduced to nonflight status within three years. The single other Lancaster headed northeast to Sweden, there to be adapted as an engine test bed.